ON TO FULL GROWTH

Encouragements and Warnings

Stephen Kaung

ISBN: 978-1-942521-02-0

Available from:

Christian Testimony Ministry
4424 Huguenot Road
Richmond, Virginia 23235

www.christiantestimonyministry.com

Printed in USA

CONTENTS

Stephen Kaung gave these messages of exhortation from the book of Hebrews in the spring of 1983 in Richmond, VA. There are at least five distinctive exhortations, complete with encouragements and warnings. We believe they are very relevant for the days in which we are living. They are transcribed and printed here by permission. All Scripture quotations are from the New Translation by J. N. Darby unless otherwise indicated.

SO GREAT SALVATION

Hebrews 13:22—But I beseech you, brethren, bear the word of exhortation, for it is but in few words that I have written to you.

Hebrews 13:22—Listen patiently and bear forth this message of exhortation and admonition and encouragement, for I have written to you briefly. (Amplified Bible)

Hebrews 2:1-4—For this reason we should give heed more abundantly to the things we have heard, lest in any way we should slip away. [Lest in any way we should drift from it and slip away] (Amplified Bible) For if the word which was spoken by angels was firm, and every transgression and disobedience received just retribution, how shall we escape if we have been negligent of so great salvation, which, having had its commencement in being spoken of by the Lord, has been confirmed to us by those who have heard; God bearing, besides, witness with them to it, both by signs and wonders, and various acts of power, and distributions of the Holy Spirit, according to his will?

Let us pray:

Dear heavenly Father, we do praise and thank Thee that by the grace of God and the redemption of our Lord Jesus we have the boldness, not only to enter into Thy presence but to remain there. And we do praise and thank Thee that now we do remain in Thy presence, and we ask that the light of Thy countenance will shine upon us and reveal to us Thy heart and draw us into Thyself. We ask in the name of our Lord Jesus. Amen.

The letter to the Hebrews is a letter of exhortation. This is clearly stated at the end of the letter where the writer says, "I beseech you, brethren, I entreat you brethren to bear with the word of exhortation, to listen patiently and bear with the message of exhortation, admonition and encouragement, because I have written you briefly" (see 13:22).

We may think that the letter to the Hebrews is a long letter, but the writer says he has written very briefly. It is not long at all if we understand what he is talking about. Hence, this letter is primarily a letter of exhortation.

Let us consider what exhortation means. It is to call to a person because the word *para* means "to the side," *kaleo* means "to call"—"to call to the side." It simply means "to entreat, to beseech, to call, to admonish, to urge someone to pursue a certain course of conduct." Therefore, exhortation in the Scripture means "to pay attention to, to warn against, and to encourage to." Therefore, we will find in this letter many encouragements and warnings.

There are at least five distinctive exhortations, complete with encouragements and warnings in this letter. The words "let us" are in there a number of times and it means encouragement or to encourage us. Then we find the word "lest" used a number of times. Whenever that word is used, it is a warning. So, there is both the negative and the positive side. Encouragement is positive; warning is negative.

The reason for these encouragements and warnings is because of the greatness of the subject, of the prospect that is found in this letter, and also because of the ease of losing it.

We will consider the first exhortation which is found in Hebrews 2:1-4. One thing worth noticing is that whenever an exhortation is given in the letter to the Hebrews, it either follows or precedes a message, a truth, a teaching, or a reality that is of tremendous importance. This is true throughout the whole book. For instance, this first exhortation stands between chapters 1 and 2. In chapter 1 we see the glory of the Son of God; in chapter 2 we see the suffering of the Son of Man. In chapter 1 we see what Christ is in eternity; in chapter 2 we see what He is in time. In chapter 1 we see especially the person of our Lord Jesus; in chapter 2 we see especially the work of our Lord Jesus. And in between these two chapters we find the first exhortation.

God Speaks

In this first exhortation the writer says, "For this reason we should give heed more abundantly to the things we have heard"

(Hebrews 2:1a). What are the things that we have heard? Certainly "these things" do not refer to those things that the prophets in the past spoke of, because chapter 1:1 says, "God having spoken in many parts and in many ways formerly to the fathers in the prophets."

God Spoke through the Prophets

Our God is a God who speaks. Thank God for that! If He should keep silent no one would know Him; no one would know what His plan is; no one would know what He is going to do. But thank God, our God is one who speaks, and in the past He spoke to our fathers through many prophets in many parts and in many ways. In other words, the prophets, being men, even though they were holy men of God, were just human beings. Therefore, they were very limited in their capacity. When God used them and the Spirit of God moved them to speak, they could only speak in parts; they could never speak in fullness. They could only speak in many ways—sometimes in parables, sometimes in types, sometimes using history, sometimes using stories. That is the way God spoke to our fathers in the prophets, but this is not what we have heard, as the writer to the Hebrews mentioned.

What is it that we have heard to which we need to pay very close attention? These are not the words spoken by the prophets, however important these words may be, but these are the words spoken by our Lord Jesus. At the end of these last days, God has spoken to us in the Person of His own Son. In the past God spoke through the prophets. It was God speaking, but He spoke through the prophets. But now, God has spoken to us in the person of His own Son, and when He speaks in His Son, it is full, rich, final, and total. That is what we have heard.

God Spoke Through the Angels

What we have heard does not refer to what the angels spoke. In Hebrews 2:2 it says, "If the word which was spoken by angels was firm ..." Now, we wonder when the angels spoke. Of course, it refers to the time when Moses received the Ten Commandments or the Law on Mount Sinai. The Bible says that when he received the word on Mount Sinai, it was through the ministration of the angels. God used the angels as His agent to speak the word to Moses, and then Moses spoke the word to the children of Israel.

However, what we have heard here does not refer to the words spoken by the angels, however important these words might be. These words have been spoken by our Lord Himself. They are not the word of law spoken by the angels, but the Word spoken by our Lord Jesus is the Word of truth and grace. How much more important is that which we have heard! If we need to hear the prophets, if we need to take heed to the words spoken by the angels, how much more we need to pay close attention to the Word spoken by the Son of God, the Lord Jesus. What has He spoken that the prophets have not spoken? What has He spoken that the angels have not spoken? This is important for us to know. What have we heard today? In verse 3 it says, "How shall we escape if we have been negligent of so great salvation?" That is it! What we have heard from the Lord Himself is so great salvation.

Forgiveness of Sins

Salvation is an all-inclusive word. Sometimes we limit salvation in our understanding to mean just having our sins forgiven, receiving eternal life, and having the promise to go to heaven. Now thank God, for these are big things to us, tremendous things. Just think of that—our sins forgiven. We who were dead in sins and transgressions—"for the wages of sin is death"—there was no hope in us. But thank God that our sins are completely forgiven—and not only forgiven but forgotten. What good news this is to us!

Eternal Life

Think of having eternal life. This natural life that we have is a mortal life, a corrupted life, a sinful life, a defeated life, and a life that is destined for death. But this new life we receive is eternal life—a life that never dies, and a life that not only continues on, but continues on in glory. Of course, that is wonderful to us.

Going to Heaven

Thank God, through the salvation of our Lord Jesus our direction is changed, and we are going to heaven. We who were destined for hell are going to heaven. Wonderful! This is the salvation that we usually understand, but is this the "so great salvation" the Lord Jesus has spoken of? So far as we are concerned it is great, but so far as God is concerned, so far as our Lord Jesus is concerned, that is not great enough for Him. The salvation that we usually hear and understand is initial salvation. We do not find this word in the Scriptures, but we use it in order to differentiate it. We might speak of it as common salvation. It is to our common knowledge that this is what salvation is. Nevertheless, if we listen to what our Lord Jesus says, we will understand that salvation is much, much greater than having our sins forgiven and receiving eternal life with a promise of going to heaven.

Salvation: Past—Present—Future

Salvation not only has something to do with the past, it has to do with the present, and of course, it has to do with the future. In Ephesians

2:5 it says, "By grace ye are saved." In the Greek original it says, "By grace ye are having been saved." That is past. In other words, when you believe in the Lord Jesus you are saved and this being saved is a settled matter. It is a thing that is done once and forever. That is salvation in the past tense: "ye are having been saved." Isn't that wonderful?

Many people who have believed in the Lord Jesus live in fear and trembling wondering whether after they die and go to the gates of heaven they will meet Moses or the Lord Jesus, whether they will be received into heaven or barred from heaven. But thank God, if we believe in the Lord Jesus, "by grace ye are having been saved." Our salvation is sure and secure; nothing can take it away from us, not even ourselves. However, this is salvation in the past tense.

In the Scriptures there is salvation in the present tense. "For the word of the cross is to them that perish foolishness, but to us that are being saved, it is the power of God" (I Corinthians 1:18).

In Romans 5:10 it says, "Having been reconciled ye shall be saved in the power of His life." And in the Amplified Version it is: "Ye shall be saved." In other words, in the present time we can be saved by being daily delivered from sin's dominion. In other words, in the present time we can be saved by being daily delivered from the power of sin. We do not need to live under the dominion of sin any more. We can overcome the law of sin and of death because now the law of the Spirit of life operates in us in Christ Jesus. That is salvation in the present tense.

Then we will find salvation in the future tense, for instance Hebrews 1:14: "Those who shall inherit salvation." Thus we see that salvation is something that we shall inherit. Whenever we think of inheritance, it is something in the future, because after the heir inherits he is no longer an heir; he is an owner. So, inheritance has something to do with the future and this is salvation.

"Blessed be the God and father of our Lord Jesus Christ, who, according to his great mercy, has begotten us again to a living hope through the resurrection of Jesus Christ from among the dead" (1 Peter 1:3).

We are begotten or born again to a living hope, and hope is something that is in the future. What is the hope? "... to an incorruptible and undefiled and unfading inheritance" (v. 4). Everything in this world is corruptible; not only corruptible but corrupted. Everything in this world is defiled; not only defilable but defiled. Everything in this world is fading or passing away; but thank God, we have a hope for an inheritance which is incorruptible. And it is not only uncorrupted, but it cannot be corrupted. It is an undefiled and unfading inheritance, "reserved in the heaven for you who are kept guarded by the power of God through faith" (v. 5). It is reserved for those who are kept by the power of God through faith. We cannot keep ourselves, but God can. However, we need to believe Him. What are they kept guarded by the power of God through faith for? "... for salvation ready to be revealed in the last time" (v. 5b). There is a salvation that is reserved for you ready to be revealed in the last time for those who are kept by the power of God through faith to inherit this salvation. This is salvation in the future.

SALVATION: SPIRIT—SOUL—BODY

Salvation is a big thing; it covers the past, present, and future. Not only that, but we are told in the Scriptures that salvation reaches to different areas of our being. We are a tripartite person, which is a man made of three parts—spirit, soul and body. "Now the God of peace himself sanctify you wholly: and your whole spirit, and soul, and body be preserved blameless at the coming of our Lord Jesus Christ" (I Thessalonians 5:23).

When we believe in the Lord Jesus, we are born again. He that is born of the Spirit is spirit—that is the salvation of the spirit. Our spirit was dead in sins and transgressions, but then it was quickened into new life. It has become a new spirit, and the Spirit of God comes and dwells in our spirit. This is regeneration, this is born again, this is salvation of the spirit.

Then the Scriptures mention the salvation of the soul, and this term is actually mentioned in the Bible. If we lose our soul today for the gospel's sake and for Christ's sake, we shall gain it to eternity. That is the salvation of the soul.

Then there is the salvation of the body or the redemption of the body. When the Lord Jesus shall come, this mortal body shall be changed into immortality; this corruptible body shall be changed into incorruptibility, and we shall have a body of glory. Today, we have a body of humiliation. This body really humiliates me, but one day we shall have a body of glory. Thank God, when that day comes, it will be the complete salvation. Therefore, salvation is "so great salvation."

The Habitable World to Come

We limit God's salvation to a corner. We think that is good enough for us; but remember, it is not good enough for God or good enough for our Lord Jesus. What He has spoken to us, what He has provided for us is "so great salvation." Therefore, we will consider together this "so great salvation" as we find within the first exhortation. Why are we exhorted to pay special attention to what we have heard, and are warned lest we slip away or drift apart? It is because of "so great salvation."

"For he has not subjected to angels the habitable world which is to come, of which we speak" (Hebrews 2:5).

What is the habitable world which is to come? In Genesis, after God had created the heavens and the earth and had restored it to be habitable in six days, on the sixth day He created man in His own image, according to His likeness. Then He blessed the man whom He created and said: "Multiply, fill the earth, have dominion over the fowls of the air, the beasts of the field and the fish of the sea" (see 1:26). In other words, after God created man in His own image, He gave him the earth to rule and subjected it to the dominion of this man whom He created; and this is God's will—of course for a reason.

God created man and put him in the habitable world and gave him dominion to rule the earth for God. What a privilege! But unfortunately, man disobeyed God. He fell into temptation and he not only lost the image of

God, but he also lost the dominion over the earth.

Today, we cannot command even a little sparrow. Oftentimes, when we see a sparrow and call it to come to us, it will not listen. And if we go towards it and try to befriend it, that sparrow will fly away. Man has lost dominion, not only over the sparrow, but also the tiger or a lion.

Man Lost Dominion

Man has lost dominion over the earth. But does it mean that God has given up His purpose concerning man because of this? Not at all, because three thousand years later, King David, as a prophet of God, wrote Psalm 8:4-5b: "What is man that Thou art mindful of him? and the son of man that thou visited him? Thou hast made him a little lower than the angels."

So far as the order of creation and man is concerned, man is a lower order than the angels because the angels are spirits. We have spirit, soul, and body, and this body really encumbers us. If we were only spirit—as the angels are—we could be everywhere, but with this body we can be only in one place. Hence, we are created a little lower than the angels. But even though man is created a little lower than angels, yet God has crowned him with glory and honor and given him dominion over the things that He has created. Now you may say that is not true anymore because man lost his inheritance or his place when he sinned. But the sweet singer of Israel, David, still continues to say in the spirit of prophecy: "What is man that Thou art mindful of him? You have not given him up. What You have purposed concerning him is still there. You are still going to let him have dominion over the earth, but it will take another thousand years."

As we come to Hebrews, chapter 2, we find the beginning of the fulfillment of God's purpose and his prophecy: "What is man that thou rememberest him, or the son of man that thou hast visited him? Thou has made him some little inferior to the angels; thou hast crowned him with glory and honor and hast set him over the works of thy hands; thou hast subjected all things under his feet. For in subjecting all things to him, he has left nothing unsubject to him. But now we see not yet all things subjected to him, but we see Jesus" (Hebrews: 2:6-9).

The Man of God's Heart

After God created Adam, for four thousand years He continued to look for the man that He created, the man of God's heart. Finally, He found that Man in Jesus. The Lord Jesus, even though He was the eternal Son of God, was made a little inferior to the angels. The Word became flesh, God incarnate, and when God became a Man, He was made a little inferior to the angels. Jesus took a place lower than the angels as a Man, but God has crowned Him with glory and honor and has subjected all things to Him. He has given all things to Him, but we have not seen this complete yet. We only see Jesus made a little lower than angels on account of the suffering of death.

Why is it that He must be made a little lower than angels? Why is it that He must be made a Man like you and me? It is because He had to suffer the suffering of death. God cannot die; He is immortal. In order for God to die He had to become a Man. The reason for His incarnation is because He wanted to suffer and die for us. Therefore, because He has tasted death for everyone, God has crowned Him with glory and honor. He is risen—He is ascended—He is anointed as Lord and Christ. God has given all things to Him and all things are going to be subjected to Him.

This is the Man; but is it just for Jesus Himself? No. If it were just for Himself, He did not need to become a Man, because as the Son of God He was crowned with glory and honor and all things were made subject to Him. That was His right, and it belonged to Him. God had given this to man and he lost it; therefore, the Lord Jesus came to regain it for God, taking it out of the hand of the enemy and restoring it to man. He did this for a new mankind, those whom He has and is going to redeem.

"He has not subjected to angels the habitable world which is to come, of which we speak" (Hebrews 2:5). The habitable world, which is to come, points to the millennium that is coming. According to Jewish usage, when they say "the habitable world to come," it means when the Messiah shall come and establish His kingdom.

MANY SONS TO GLORY

What is "so great salvation"? Christ has come! He has taken this earth out of the hands of the usurper, Satan, and brought it back to Himself and to those whom He has redeemed that they may inherit that incorruptible, undefiled and unfading inheritance. To use one word to describe it—Glory! "For it became him, for whom are all things, and by whom are all things, in bringing many sons to glory, to make perfect the leader of their salvation through sufferings" (Hebrews 2:10).

The writer of Hebrews uses the word "their salvation;" and that salvation means glory. It is not just a matter of having our sins forgiven. Of course, having sins upon us is shameful, condemnable, despicable, and having our sins forgiven is a very joyous experience, that is true. However, what God has in mind for us is far greater than just having our sins forgiven; He is going to lead us into glory. Christ is now in glory, and one day He is going to bring many sons to glory—to share His glory, to share His reign, to share His throne, to rule upon this earth over all things as heirs and co-heirs with Christ. How glorious this is!

How is He going to bring many sons to glory? He has already gone to glory; but He went through suffering to be made perfect as the Leader of their salvation. It was through His suffering that He was perfected. He is perfect, and yet He needed to be perfected.

Hebrews 5 says, "Though He was Son, He learned obedience from the things which He suffered that He may be our eternal salvation" (see vv. 8-9a). The Lord Jesus has not only provided for us a salvation, He has also opened a way to this salvation which is through suffering.

United With the Lord Jesus

"For both He that sanctifies and those sanctified are all of one; for which cause He is not ashamed to call them brethren" (Hebrews 2:11).

He that sanctifies is the Lord Jesus, and we are the ones who are sanctified. We are united with Him; therefore, we are all of one. First, He came to be united with us. We are of flesh and blood; so He partook of flesh and blood to be united with us in order that He might die for us. Now, He has united us together with Himself. He that sanctifies and those that are sanctified are all of one, and He calls us brethren. How wonderful it is that He calls us brothers—male brothers and female brothers! We are all brothers to Him because we share His life; we are His brethren. "I will declare thy name to my brethren; in the midst of the assembly will I sing thy praises" (Hebrews 2:12).

We are His assembly, His church. Through His death and resurrection we are united with Christ. Thus He says, "Go to my brethren and say to them, I ascend to my Father and your Father; and to my God and your God" (John 20:17).

We become His blood brothers and His assembly which is His church. He will sing praises in the assembly; we become His children that God has given to Him. By believing in the Lord Jesus, we are His children—not just babes.

We begin as babes, but He is to lead many sons into glory.

Grown-up Sons and Daughters

When we believe in the Lord Jesus, we become children of God, babes in Christ. But we are not to remain as babes, because if we do, then God's purpose for us cannot be realized. God wants us to rule and reign with Christ in glory. He wants to put all things under our feet just as He has subjected all things under the feet of Christ. Can He do that if we are just babes? We cannot manage as babes; we need to grow up into sonship. God wants grown-up sons and daughters; therefore, we need to grow up.

What does it mean to "grow up"? It means that the measure of Christ in us has to be increased. Christ has to increase in us and we decrease—then we are growing into sonship. And one day, at the manifestation of the sons of God the whole earth will be transformed.

The earth today is in groaning because it is subject to corruption and vanity. The whole world is vanity of vanity—no purpose. The whole earth is corrupted—everything is corrupted. For instance, look at the trees. They have many leaves in the springtime and it is wonderful, but it does not last long. The fall and winter come and the trees are bare; they are corrupted. Everything is vain with no purpose. Not only is there no purpose to human beings, but there is no purpose to anything in the world. The whole creation is subject to vanity and corruption.

Who subjects the whole creation into vanity and corruption? Man. But one day when the sons of God shall be manifested, when the Son of God shall lead many sons into glory, when the only Begotten shall be the firstborn among His many brethren, then the whole world will be restored. This is "so great salvation." It is nothing less than this.

GIVE HEED TO WHAT WE HAVE HEARD

This is so thrilling when we consider it. Think of the "so great salvation" that Christ has spoken of, that He has provided for and called us into. And because of the greatness of the theme and the subject, we are encouraged and exhorted to give heed more abundantly to the things we have heard. We need to pay much closer attention to what we have heard. Many people hear but they do not hear because their heart is not there.

In the parable of the sower, we will recall that when the Word is being scattered, some seed falls into the pathway being trodden hard by feet. In other words, the traffic of the world is so heavy that the heart is hardened by the things of the world and the seed just cannot enter into it. He may hear but he does not hear. And the birds or the wicked one (see Matthew 13:19) will come and take the seed away, and it is as if he had not heard.

Or one's heart may be like stony ground. When there is stone underneath a very thin layer of earth, and the seed falls into that earth and begins to come forth, there is no root. When there is tribulation, this one will fall away.

Or it may be like a ground with thorns. The seed goes in and begins to come up, but it can bear no fruit because the weeds, the thorns, or the thistles take away all the nutrition. We know that thorns are aborted fruit that do not come to fruition.

It is only the ground or that heart that has been tilled, turned over, softened, and prepared that the Word can fall into and patiently bear fruit a hundredfold, sixtyfold, and thirtyfold to the glory of God. Dear brothers and sisters, may we pay close attention to what we hear. Be careful lest our hearts are not in it, and we hear as if we have not heard.

MORE ABUNDANTLY

This phrase, "more abundantly" is used a second time in chapter 6:17: "Wherein God, willing to shew more abundantly to the heirs of the promise the unchangeableness of his purpose, intervened by an oath."

Here, the "more abundantly" is on God's side. He wants to show us the immutability, the unchangeableness of His purpose, so He gives us more abundantly His proofs. He even makes an oath. Whatever God says is true. He does not need to take an oath, but He takes an oath in order to encourage us more abundantly. Surely we need to pay more abundant attention to such "more abundant grace." Let us hear.

Lest We Slip Away

"Lest in any way we should slip away" (Hebrews 2:1). This word "slip away" has been explained in three different ways. The original Greek is very rich, but when you translate it into English you can only put one shade of meaning in it.

A Leaking Vessel

Some say this word means "running out" just like a leaking vessel. Suppose you have a vessel that has holes in it and you try to draw water with it. You go to the river and draw water and try to bring it home, but when you get home it is all gone because it has all leaked out. Be careful lest what you have heard leak out and run out.

How often this is true! We come to a meeting and hear the Word of God spoken, but after we step out of the door, if anybody should ask us what we have heard, we cannot remember. It has all leaked out. Isn't it strange that we can remember lots of things, but when it comes to the things of God, we just cannot remember? We need to be careful lest all that we have heard has run out from a leaking vessel. Oh, that we be not leaking vessels—hearing a lot but retaining very little! It has all leaked. It does not produce what it should. Oh, how we need to be careful before God!

Slip Away

Another way to put it is: "slip away." We have often said: "Well, it just slipped my mind. I just do not remember." Why does it slip your mind? In the first place it is because your heart is not in it. If your heart were really in it, it could not slip nor would it slip away. Why do you remember lots of things? It is because your heart is in it.

Suppose somebody does something wrong to us. We can never forget because it touches our heart; we remember it. But when somebody does something good to us, we can easily forget; we take it for granted. May we be careful lest in any way it slips away from us. Because it can slip away, therefore hold it tightly.

How do we hold it tightly? When we hear the Word of God and just go away, it is almost like what you find in the book of James. People look at the mirror and then turn away and forget how they look. Many people are like that. We hear the Word and go home, and it all slips away. How can we hold on to it and fix it in our hearts? Mingle it with faith and pray through it. That will hold it and fix it so it will not just slip away. That is why it is always good after a message that we pray over it in order to hold it and get it fixed in our hearts. Even after we go home we should think about it, ponder over it, and pray over it so that it will be fixed in our hearts. Then it will never slip away.

Drift Apart

Another way of putting it is "drift apart." It is like a ship that is in the water. The ship is sailing toward a haven, and then there is a storm. If we do not put forth effort to sail the ship and we just let it drift, the wind and the storm will blow the ship away from the haven where we want to arrive. We will just drift away. How true it is that oftentimes we cannot reach or attain to what

God has provided for us because we make no effort at all; we just let our lives drift.

If we allow our lives to drift, the current will take us away from God; not unto God. A live fish has to swim against the current. When it flows with the current, we know it is a dead fish. Let us not drift, because if we do, we will miss the haven.

The terrible thing with drifting is that it does not occur suddenly. Drifting is something that goes on in our lives day by day, hour by hour, unknowingly. We can picture it as a man in a canoe, paddling in a lake that joins to Niagara Falls. He finds the water very smooth there and the sun so warm that he begins to drop his paddle, lie back and let the canoe drift. He thinks everything is fine until suddenly he comes to the edge of the falls—and it is too late! That is drifting.

Our Christian life cannot afford to drift. This "so great salvation" that God has given to us is so precious we cannot afford to let it slip away. We cannot let it leak out but we are to lay hold of it. It is as the Bible says, "Lay hold on eternal life."

NEGLIGENCE

Why do we slip? Why do we drift? It is because we are being negligent. We do not need to commit something terrible; all we need do is to neglect it, and we lose it.

In addition to Hebrews 2:3, "How shall we escape if we neglect so great salvation," the word neglect is used three other places in the New Testament. The Lord said: "Because they did not continue in my covenant I did not regard them" (Hebrews 8:9).

The word *disregard* in the original is the same word as the word *neglect*. God said: "I will neglect My covenant because they have first violated My covenant."

A covenant is between two parties and when one party has violated the terms of the covenant, the other party has every right just to neglect it, to declare it as null and void; and that is what God did. He declared the old covenant as null and void; He neglected it. So neglect does not mean just being careless, but a deliberate putting aside of what we should pay attention to or what we should perform.

Do not think that neglect is just carelessness. Sometimes neglect is being careless, that is true; but, sometimes neglect is more than being careless—it is deliberate. How sinful it is if we deliberately neglect "so great salvation" spoken to us by the Son of God, endorsed by the heavenly Father, established by the Holy Spirit. How sinful this must be! How can we deliberately disregard or neglect "so great salvation"?

Continual Negligence

"Be not negligent of the gift that is in thee, which has been given to thee through prophecy, with imposition of the hands of the elderhood" (I Timothy 4:14). Here the word "negligent" has the sense of continuation. In other words, it is not just neglecting it once, but if you continually neglect it, it becomes a habit. Negligence can become a habit because if you neglect it again and again and again, the thing is gone. If you neglect the gift that God has given you the first time the Holy Spirit moves you to exercise it, then you neglect it the second time, and you continue to neglect it, it is as if you no longer have it.

"But they made light of it" (Matthew 22:5). A marriage feast was provided and the people were invited, but they made light of it—that is neglect. They considered other things as more important. They considered their oxen which they had bought more important; they considered the field that they had bought more important; they considered the wife they had married more important than the Son, the King. If we make light of what Christ has spoken to us—"so great salvation"—we neglect it. Do not make light of it. Give it your first priority.

Andrew Murray once said: "The feebleness and sickliness of the Christian life, today, is because we do not pay intense attention, close attention, or give priority to God and to His Word."

Just Retribution

This is the first exhortation and the tremendous greatness of the theme "so great salvation." We are encouraged to pay close attention. We are warned not to neglect it. How shall we escape if we neglect it? We not only miss it, which means that we will not be able to enter into glory and reign with Christ for a thousand years during the millennium, but worse than that, it says, "How shall you escape?" Escape what? To lose something is one thing; it is bad enough, but not to escape something terrible is another thing. What is it that you shall not escape?

The words spoken by the angels are the words of the Law. If anyone should violate the word of the Law, he will receive just retribution. When we see in the Old Testament those people who disobeyed and transgressed the law of God and what happened to them, it was "just retribution." They are paid back what they deserve. How shall we escape if we have been negligent of "so great salvation"? The principle is this: the greater the privilege, the greater the responsibility and the greater the retribution. Think of that and be warned of it. May the Lord have mercy upon us.

Shall we pray:

Dear heavenly Father, oh our hearts do cry out to Thee. What grace, what mercy, what salvation Thou hast spoken and provided for us! Oh, that we may hear, we may see, we may take to heart, that we may pay close attention to and give our lives to it that we may not lose it, let it slip away, run out, or drift past. Lord, we pray that we may not be negligent people but we may be a people who are diligent towards Thyself. We ask in the name of our Lord Jesus. Amen.

THE HEAVENLY CALLING

Hebrews 3:1-14—Wherefore, holy brethren, partakers of the heavenly calling, consider the Apostle and High Priest of our confession, Jesus, who is faithful to him that has constituted him, as Moses also in all his house. For he has been counted worthy of greater glory than Moses, by how much he that has built it has more honor than the house. For every house is built by some one; but he who has built all things is God. And Moses indeed was faithful in all his house, as a ministering servant, for a testimony of the things to be spoken after; but Christ, as Son over his house, whose house are we, if indeed we hold fast the boldness and the boast of hope firm to the end. Wherefore, even as says the Holy Spirit, Today if ye will hear his voice, harden not your hearts, as in the provocation, in the day of temptation in the wilderness; where your fathers tempted me, by proving me, and saw my works forty years. Wherefore I was wroth with this generation, and said, They always err in heart; and they have not known my ways; so I swore in my wrath, If they shall enter into my rest. See, brethren, lest there be in any one of you a wicked heart of unbelief, in turning away from the living God. But encourage yourselves each day, as long as it is called Today, that none of you be hardened by the deceitfulness of sin. For we are become companions of the Christ if indeed we hold the beginning of the assurance firm to the end.

Hebrews 4:1—Let us therefore fear, lest, a promise being left of entering into his rest, any one of you might seem to have failed of it.

Hebrews 4:11—Let us therefore use diligence to enter into that rest, that no one may fall after the same example of not hearkening to the word.

Let us pray:

Dear heavenly Father, we do commit Thy own Word back into Thy hands, and ask Thee to bless it and break it and give to each one of us that we may be full. We ask in the name of our Lord Jesus. Amen.

The second exhortation is found in chapters 3 and 4 of Hebrews. The great theme that is before us is found in 3:1: "Wherefore, holy brethren, partakers of the heavenly calling ..." The children of Israel received a calling from God, but it was an earthly calling. We, who are the redeemed of the Lord, have received a calling from God and it is a heavenly calling because we are a heavenly people of God.

What is a calling? What has God called us into? The calling that comes from God constitutes our vocation. It becomes our life-long occupation. It is something that we must be fully committed to and totally occupied with. A calling will not only show us our destiny, it will also give us direction for that destiny. God has called us with a heavenly calling. We are partakers of a heavenly calling, and the word *partakers* means "sharers." We share that heavenly calling together.

In chapters 3 and 4 of the book of Hebrews we will find three things mentioned that form this heavenly calling. Number one, we are called to be the house of God. "But Christ, as Son over His house, whose house are we, if indeed we hold fast the boldness and the boast of hope firm to the end" (Hebrews 3:6).

Number two, we are called to be the companions of Christ, and the word "companions" is the same word as the word "partakers" in Hebrews 3:1. "For we are become companions of the Christ if indeed we hold the beginning of the assurance firm to the end" (Hebrews 3:14).

Number three, we are called to enter into His rest. "Let us therefore fear, lest, a promise being left of entering into his rest, any one of you might seem to have failed of it" (Hebrews 4:1).

HOUSE OF GOD

We are called to be the house of God. We are not only being justified, we are not only being glorified, we are not only as many sons whom the Son will lead into glory individually, but we are called corporately to be the house of God. This is our heavenly calling. Can you find any calling more heavenly and more spiritual than this?

It is the eternal desire of God to dwell among men. After He redeemed the children of Israel out of Egypt, He brought them to Mount Sinai where He gave them His Law. He also commanded Moses to build Him a tabernacle because this was to be His dwelling place among the children of Israel. How much better it is today that God does not dwell in a physical tabernacle in order to live among His people. Instead, God has made His people His home; therefore, He dwells directly in and among His own people. He has called us to be His house, His holy habitation, His spiritual house. That is our heavenly calling.

But let us take note of one little word in verse 6—*if*. Whenever you find the word *if*, it means that we are not dealing with this matter objectively as truth. It is objectively true, but when the word *if* is there, we know we are now entering into the realm of subjective experience.

High privilege demands great responsibility—the higher the privilege, the greater the responsibility. We are so privileged to be called the house of God—that God would dwell in our midst, God would find His rest in us, God's heart would be satisfied with us, that God would be loved and worshipped and served by His people. This is a tremendous privilege, but because the privilege is so high the responsibility is very great. That is why the word *if* is there. We are God's house *if*..."

Do not think that the house of God comes automatically—because you are saved, therefore you are the house of God. Not so! One stone, even if it is a living stone, is not a house. These living stones have to be built up together in order to be a house and that is where our responsibility is.

It is true that our Lord Jesus said: "I will build my church upon this rock." It is the Lord Himself who builds the house. He is not only a Son over His house, but He is also the builder of the house. He is going to build the believers together as living stones upon Himself as the foundation to be a holy habitation for God. That is the work that our Lord Jesus will do. But we must remember that He is going to build us up. Unless we are willing to yield ourselves into His hand and co-operate with Him, He will not be able to build us together in Himself. That is why the word *if* is there—"... whose house are we, if indeed we hold fast the boldness and the boast of hope firm to the end."

What is our hope? Our hope is that one day we will be the finished house of God so that God can dwell among us eternally. God can make us His eternal home and then we will find our eternal home in Him. This is our hope. "Let us hold fast the boldness and the boast of our hope firm to the end." In other words, this is our boast; this is our boldness that one day we will become the completed house of God. Hold fast to that, and do not give it up easily because in the very process of building us together there is much chiseling, cutting, sawing, smoothing, refining, and reducing. In other words, there is much work to be done in our lives which is the cross. Because there is such a working of the cross in our life, sometimes we get disappointed, or discouraged, or we faint and want to draw back or flee away. Therefore, we refuse to cooperate and we give up our hope. And if we do, then the Lord is not able to build us into His house or build us together. That is the why the word *if* is there.

Dear brothers and sisters, how can we hold fast the boldness and the boast of hope to the end? Here is the secret: "Christ in you, the hope of glory." In other words, it is because Christ is in you. As a matter of fact, Christ is not taking you and me as the building blocks of the house; He is actually taking Himself in you and me to build up the house of God. The reason you and I have to be eliminated is that He may be increased and we be decreased in order that the house may be built. Thank God, "Christ in you the hope of glory." In me, that is in my flesh there is no good. If it depends upon me, not only will I fail, but God will have to give up. Thank God, it does not depend on me! It depends on the Christ in me and because He is in me, He is the hope of glory. One day, that house will be built and this is our heavenly calling.

COMPANIONS OF CHRIST

We are companions or active partners of Christ. We are to be full partners; not as some people say "sleeping partners"—which means we are partners but not active at all. We are to be actively engaged together in the business Christ came to earth to do.

We like to share with Christ in having our sins forgiven and in the gift of eternal life. In other words, we like to share with Christ in what we call common salvation or initial salvation. But how many brothers and sisters are willing to be living partners with Christ in His business and in the very purpose that Christ came to fulfill?

The reason Christ came into the world is to build His house in order that He may have a body and when that body is fully grown, He may have His bride. Now that is the business that Christ is engaged with. Are we actively involved in that business?

The apostle Paul said: "I rejoice in suffering for you because I am filling up the affliction of

Christ concerning His body" (see Colossians 1:24). Are we just interested in our own interest? Are we interested only in going to heaven? Of course, we are interested, but has that become our sole interest? Or are we taken up with the interest of Christ? Are we just concerned with our welfare or are we concerned with the welfare of God? If we are concerned with the welfare of God, then we become active partners with Christ and companions of Christ. One day, those who accompany Christ on earth today will become His companions when He will be crowned and receive His bride.

In Psalm 45, which is a prophecy of the marriage of the king and the queen, it is also a prophecy concerning the union of Christ and His church. God has anointed Him with the oil of gladness above His companions. This tells us that there will be companions there, but let us remember that only those who follow the Lamb wheresoever He goes will become His companions at His marriage feast. We need to hold fast the assurance of our hope firm to the end. Again the word *if* is there; it is a great responsibility.

Entering Into His Rest

The third thing spoken of in the heavenly calling is this matter of entering into His rest. When the children of Israel were in Egypt there was no rest because they were slaves and were put in hard labor. They were in a fiery furnace. They were not even going to be allowed to live; the whole race was to be eliminated. BUT GOD—delivered them out of Egypt with the purpose of leading them into Canaan which meant rest for them. God wanted to lead them into rest that they might dwell in the land in safety and in peace, enjoying the land that was flowing with milk and honey. This was God's purpose concerning His people.

While God was leading them to Canaan, unfortunately, even though He proved Himself to them many times that He was faithful, that He was true to His Word, that there was nothing too hard for Him, and that He loved them, yet this people rebelled in their hearts. They hardened their hearts toward God and refused to believe His Word. They even questioned God's love and faithfulness. Therefore, even though God endured them and suffered long with them, finally, when they arrived at Kadesh-Barnea, that was the end. There came a point when God said: "Because this generation erred in their hearts, they do not know My ways, and they have provoked Me again and again and again, this generation cannot enter into My rest."

The Work is Finished

We have a promise of entering into God's rest. What is rest? And how do we enter into His rest? We cannot rest if the work is not finished, but when the work is finished, then we can rest.

God used six days to repair the earth, and on the seventh day He rested from His work, because the work was done. Even though man was created on the sixth day, actually the first day that man lived was the seventh day. In other words, it was God's purpose that man was to be created on the sixth day and immediately enter into God's rest. But unfortunately, man sinned, and he not only lost that rest in God, but God lost His rest.

Immediately after man sinned, God came to the garden to seek and to find the lost: "Adam, where are you?" God began to work and that is the reason the Lord Jesus spoke to the Pharisees as He did after He healed on the Sabbath day. The Pharisees said: "The Sabbath day is a day of rest; you should not heal anybody." The Lord said, "My Father works until now and I work." In other words, where there is sin there is no rest; therefore, God had no rest. He has to work until the work is done; then He will rest. Thank God, on Calvary's cross the last word that our Lord Jesus shouted in victory was: "It is finished!" The work is done and because the work was done on Calvary's cross, today our Lord Jesus sits at the right hand of God because the work is done. The work of redemption is finished; therefore, we are called to enter into His rest. We are to rest in His rest, which means we are to rest in the finished work of Christ.

Why is it that we are so restless? When the children of Israel were in the wilderness, they were restless. That whole picture is of a person who is living according to the flesh. We are born of the Spirit, and yet daily we still live according to the flesh, even though we try to live according to the good flesh and not the bad. Flesh is not all bad; there is the good flesh and the bad flesh. The bad flesh commits sin and the good flesh tries to please God or appease God or bribe God. As long as we are trying to live in the flesh, we become restless. As a result of this, we strive, we struggle, we strain, we stretch, and we keep trying. But in me, that is in my flesh, there is no good. Then we begin to murmur, or doubt, or lose heart, and begin to distrust God. Then we find ourselves in the wilderness where there is no rest.

Our rest is in Christ, who is Canaan to us, and His finished work. The reason we do not have rest is because we do not believe. We believe in ourselves more than we believe in Him and what He has done for us. The moment we enter into the finished work of Christ our soul enters into rest. In Matthew 11:28 the Lord Jesus said, "Come to me, all ye who labor and are heavy laden and I will give you rest."

When we were in sins and transgressions, we had no rest and the Lord said: "Come unto Me;

just come to Me all you who labor and are heavy laden, and I will give you rest. I will take away your burden and the load you are carrying, because I have already taken it upon Myself when I was on the cross." In *Pilgrim's Progress,* that pilgrim fled from the city of destruction and came to the cross, and as he looked at the cross the burden on his back rolled away.

Take My Yoke

Thank God, we who believe in the Lord Jesus have that rest in our spirit. But the Lord said there is another rest: "Take my yoke upon you, and learn from me; for I am meek and lowly in heart; and ye shall find rest to your souls" (Matthew 11:29).

Thank God, when we come to the Lord Jesus with heavy burdens, He gives us rest in the spirit and it is there forever. But unfortunately, oftentimes we are still in the wilderness, and our soul is still restless because we do not take His yoke upon us.

What is the yoke of Christ? It is the will of God. The Lord Jesus said: "Lo, I come to do Your will." The Lord took upon Himself the will of God as His yoke to control and guide Him. He took it willingly, voluntarily, happily, joyfully, and victoriously. When He put that yoke upon Himself, He was meek and lowly in heart. There was no resistance or fighting against the Father's will: "Not My will, but Your will be done." He was selfless, and He yielded Himself completely to the Father. He accomplished the will of God!

This is why He can say, "Take My yoke upon you and learn from Me." This yoke has two holes. On the one side is the Lord Jesus and He yokes us to the other side, because we are like the unbroken oxen or horse. He is going to break us by yoking us with the One who has been broken, who is always broken, and when He puts us with Christ in His field, may we learn of Him. Look at Him! When you are restless, look at Him. When you rebel, look at Him. When you feel it is too hard, look at Him.

When we do this, we will find rest in our soul because we enter into the good of His finished work. This is our calling—into His rest.

I am just explaining it spiritually. Actually, in reading this more closely, we see that rest here is His rest, and not our rest. When we learn of Him, we do enter into rest in our soul, but the whole point here is His rest. We have the promise of entering into His rest which means that when everything He wants to do is done, then He will rest. That happens during the millennial kingdom, and at that time He will have His bride. At that time He will rest in His own rest and we will rest with Him. So spiritually, the rest is something we should experience daily, even today, but dispensationally it is a promise that is before us, and if we use diligence we will enter into His rest. We will reign and rule with Christ for a thousand years.

These three things compose our heavenly calling. We are called to be the house of God, but in order to be the house of God experientially and not just positionally, we have to yield ourselves to His hand and let Him build us. We are called to be the companions of Christ, and if we want to be His companions, then we have to be actively engaged in His business. We are called to enter into His rest but to do so we have to take His yoke upon us. If we do that, one day we shall rest in His rest in the millennial kingdom.

ENCOURAGEMENT

This is the theme that is before us. Can you think of anything greater than these things? This is the heavenly calling. With such a heavenly calling, the writer wants to encourage us. He says: "Having this before us what should we do?"

Consider

"Consider the Apostle and High Priest of our confession, Jesus." The English word *consider* comes from the Latin word which is the word for "star" and the root of that word is "astronomer." He looks at the star; he considers, contemplates, gazes patiently, persistently, with concentration. He gazes at the stars and tries to discover the stars in the sky. That is the meaning of the word *consider*. Therefore in the spiritual realm it means that we should gaze upon the Lord Jesus, fix our gaze upon Him, contemplate Him, think about Him, ponder over Him, and concentrate our thought in Him.

We are to consider Him as the Apostle of our confession. The Lord Jesus is the Apostle of our confession. An apostle is one who is sent on a mission. The Lord Jesus is God's Apostle, and He was sent on a mission to build the house of God.

Moses was an apostle to the children of Israel, and he was called to build God a house, a tabernacle so that God might dwell among His people. And Moses was faithful in all His house. But here we are told that the Lord Jesus is God's Apostle, not only to the children of Israel, but to the whole world. He is to gather out of every nation, every tongue, and every tribe a people to be built together into the house of God. He is not only the builder; He is also the owner of the house. How much greater is He than Moses!

The Lord calls us, justifies us, glorifies us in order to build us together to be His house. He says, "I will build my house upon this rock (that is Himself as the foundation), and the gates of Hades shall not prevail against it" (see Matthew 16:18). There is a spiritual conflict going on over the building, but thank God, the victory is already won and the gates of Hades shall not prevail against it. In other words, He will have His house. He has overcome all the forces of His enemy on Calvary's cross. He has delivered us out of the power of darkness and has translated us into the kingdom of the Son of God's love. He has done everything, He has provided everything and He is able to save us to the uttermost. He is a High Priest, ministering to us day by day in heaven that He may save us to the uttermost. Let us consider Him, and even though it may seem impossible with us, nothing is impossible with Him. That is how our boast and boldness are kept to the end. Consider Him because it is not something you and I can do. All work is done by Him, our Apostle; all we need do is hand ourselves over to Him and let Him do it. Are we willing to do that?

Consider Jesus, the Apostle of our confession. He has already entered behind the veil as the forerunner. There is a Man in heaven sitting at the right hand of God and that Man is beckoning us to heaven. That gives us hope. He has opened the way for us and is calling us to join Him. This

Son is to lead many sons into glory, and He is determined to build us together that the gates of Hades shall not prevail against it. He will do it. Are we willing to trust Him?

Encourage One Another

"But encourage yourselves each day, as long as it is called Today, that none of you be hardened by the deceitfulness of sin" (Hebrews 3:13).

First, let us consider Jesus and then let us encourage one another. Do not consider your brothers and sisters first. If you consider your brothers and sisters first before you consider Christ, all you will receive is the weakness and the faults of your brothers and sisters. A brother once said: "I have considered that brother with a microscope." We need to consider our brothers and sisters with a telescope. However, let us consider Jesus, and if we use a microscope that is fine. But after we have considered Him, then we are to encourage one another because we are to be the house of God. It is not a matter of you and Him alone; it is a matter of you and Him and the brothers and sisters. Do not think of your own spirituality alone. Think of your brothers and sisters. Let us encourage our brothers and sisters because if they should fail the house will be delayed. It takes all of us together to build up the house and to be companions of Christ. Christ does not have just one companion; He has many.

Therefore, we need to encourage one another daily, as long as it is today. Thank God, today is the day that God has made. Let us rejoice in it. I always thank God for today. Oftentimes I tell God, "Lord, I thank You that You have given me another day—a day of opportunity." As long as there is a day which is called today, there is hope. The Spirit of God still has a chance to work and we still have a chance to let Him work. So as long as it is today, let us encourage one another daily, lest any one should fail.

Let Us Fear

"Let us therefore fear, lest, a promise being left of entering into his rest, any one of you might seem to have failed of it" (Hebrews 4:1).

Holy fear is an important ingredient in love. It is true that in I John it says, "Perfect love casts out fear;" but the fear there means the fear of punishment and perfect love casts out that kind of fear. But the Scripture says, "The fear of the Lord is the beginning of wisdom." In other words, there is a holy fear which is an important ingredient in love. Now if we love a person are we fearful? We are not afraid of being punished, but we are fearful lest we displease him. We want to please him so much that we are in fear, and that is a kind of holy fear.

Today, people are so careless, so loose. Sometimes our relationship with the Lord is too intimate. Of course, in one sense we cannot be too intimate with the Lord. But in another sense, sometimes it is a little bit unholy because of a lack of fear, as if we can do anything we want to and it does not matter. After all, He loves us, so what matters? Do we have that holy fear?—the fear that we may miss out; we may miss His purpose; we may displease Him; we may fail Him. It is nothing if we fail, but to fail Him—that makes a great difference. Are we afraid of that?

Diligence

"Let us therefore use diligence to enter into that rest" (Hebrews 4:11). Now, is that not a contradiction? On one hand, we are to enter into rest, but on the other hand, we are to exercise diligence and that means using some energy which is not resting. Wherein is that diligence to enter into that rest? We find it in the following verses: "The word of God is sharper than a two-edged sword" (v. 12). It penetrates, it cuts asunder, it divides the bone and marrow, the spirit and the soul, and it reveals the intents and thoughts of the heart for there is nothing that is not naked and laid bare before His eyes. In other words, "using diligence to enter into His rest" simply means to exercise our will to lie on the altar as a living sacrifice. Do not get off; do not struggle. Let the Priest, the Holy Spirit, use the knife, the living word of God, to divide our soul and spirit, and when our soul is divided from our spirit we enter into His rest. It is not our working but it is using diligence to lay there and not move. That is where the diligence is.

WARNINGS

Unbelief

We have looked at the encouragements, now we come to the warnings. We find that the warnings are being given because of the greatness of these things. "See brethren, lest there be in any one of you a wicked heart of unbelief in turning away from the living God" (Hebrews 3:12). Remember, these words are spoken to believers. This wicked heart of unbelief can happen to a believer. Take careful note of this. The example is used of the children of Israel (Psalm 95), who were delivered out of Egypt and then provoked the Lord in the wilderness. They did not believe in Him, they tested Him, they proved Him, they erred in heart, and they did not know His way. This happened to the delivered children of Israel, and thus this warning is to believers—brethren: "See brethren, be careful brethren, lest there be in any one of you a wicked heart of unbelief." "If any one thinks that he can stand, let him be careful lest he fall" (see I Corinthians 10:12).

Our relationship with the Lord is a matter of the heart. God has created us with a heart, and with this heart we are to fellowship with God in faith and in love. But unfortunately, this heart became a heart of stone, a stony heart through the deceitfulness of sin. Sin has deceived us and made our hearts as hard as stone; it is very deceitful. We recall how the serpent tempted Eve and how deceitful he was. It seems that the serpent suggested something that was very insignificant; just a matter of eating a fruit. What is the big issue with eating a fruit? He suggested that they would be wise, they would be clever, they would be like God—so many promises.

Sin is very deceitful. When sin comes, it deceives people. It tries to lure people into thinking there is so much pleasure in it, but it is a lie. It offers so much, as if it will satisfy you, and sometimes it seems so insignificant, such a small thing. Maybe it is just a little worldliness, a little pride, or a little jealously. It is something insignificant, but if you yield to it that sin begins to loom bigger and bigger until you are under the dominion of it, and your heart becomes hard as stone towards God. You are not able to hear

Him anymore. You will not be moved by His voice anymore, and that is what the human heart had become. There was no fellowship between man and God because the heart was stony.

But thank God, when we are convicted by the Holy Spirit and we come to the Lord Jesus, God takes away our stony heart and gives us a heart of flesh (see Ezekiel 36:26). A heart of flesh simply means that it is a living heart, a tender heart, a feeling heart, a heart that can be touched and moved by God, and can hear His voice. Our heart is the ear that hears Him, the eyes that see Him, and the capacity to receive His communication.

It is possible, even with this heart of flesh, not to hear His voice today, and tomorrow another today, and tomorrow another today. If we do not hear His voice now while the Spirit of God is speaking to us, it may become hardened. We may have a heart of flesh and He is able to speak to us, but do we listen? If we do not listen, if we do not obey, if we do not cooperate, our heart gets hardened a little bit, and the next day if we do not listen, it gets hardened further.

Finally, we may so harden our heart that it becomes a wicked heart of unbelief. We just will not believe; therefore, we do not mix faith with His word, we do not yield to His voice. The result is that we turn away from the living God.

Dear brothers and sisters, high is our privilege! Great is our responsibility! That is the reason we have to encourage one another lest someone among us gets deceived by sin. In the beginning it may be a very small, insignificant thing. It may not be a very blatant sin. It may be something very small and hidden, but when the Holy Spirit speaks to our heart, do we yield to Him? Do we believe in God's Word? Do we let God's word cut off that sin? If we harden our heart, it will get harder and harder and harder until it becomes a wicked heart of unbelief. May the Lord deliver us from such a wicked heart of unbelief. Verse 13 says, "... that none of you be hardened by the deceitfulness of sins."

Come Short

"Let us therefore fear, lest a promise being left of entering into his rest, any one of you might seem to have failed of it" (Hebrews 4:1).

You failed it; that means, "come short of it." It is God's will that we should enter into His rest today and in the millennium to come; but if we fail it, if we fall short of it, we cannot blame Him. The first generation children of Israel failed in the wilderness. They did not enter into Canaan because of their unbelief, but thank God, there were Joshua and Caleb. They had a more excellent spirit. They believed in God and believed in His Word, and they entered into the Promised Land.

May we not be like those who failed in the wilderness, who came short of God's purpose, but may we be like Caleb and Joshua, mingling faith with the Word we hear that we may enter into His rest. "That no one may fall after the same example of not hearkening to the word" (Hebrews 4:11); that we will not fall by the wayside, that we may continue on until we enter into His rest.

Thank God, He has not only put before us a tremendous calling, a heavenly calling, but He has made every provision for us to make it. He is the Apostle and the High Priest of our confession and we are to encourage one another. Every provision is there. Let us make use of His provision and not harden our hearts through the deceitfulness of sin and develop a wicked heart of unbelief that will cause us to fall and fail and come short of the purpose of God.

Shall we pray:

Dear heavenly Father, how we do praise and thank Thee that Thou hast called us with a heavenly calling, and what a calling it is! Thou wants us to be Thy house, Thy companion, and into Thy rest. Oh Father, we just desire it very much, and we do praise and thank Thee that Thou dost call us to consider Jesus, the Apostle and High Priest of our confession, and Thou dost also encourage us to encourage and exhort one another daily as it is today, that we, by Thy grace, may make it. Oh our Father, do be merciful to us, that none of us will fall by the wayside, but we may all enter into that rest that Thou hast provided for us. And we praise and worship Thee in the name of our Lord Jesus. Amen.

PERFECTION

Hebrews 5:1-6:12—For every high priest taken from amongst men is established for men in things relating to God, that he may offer both gifts and sacrifices for sins; being able to exercise forbearance towards the ignorant and erring, since he himself also is clothed with infirmity; and, on account of this infirmity, he ought, even as for the people, so also for himself, to offer for sins. And no one takes the honour to himself but as called by God, even as Aaron also. Thus the Christ also has not glorified himself to be made a high priest; but he who had said to him, Thou art my Son, I have to-day begotten thee. Even as also in another place he says, Thou art a priest for ever according to the order of Melchisedec. Who in the days of his flesh, having offered up both supplications and entreaties to him who was able to save him out of death, with strong crying and tears; (and having been heard because of his piety;) though he were Son, he learned obedience from the things which he suffered; and having been perfected, became to all them that obey him, author of eternal salvation; addressed by God as high priest according to the order of Melchisedec. Concerning whom we have much to say, and hard to be interpreted in speaking of it, since ye are become dull in hearing. For when for the time ye ought to be teachers, ye have again need that one should teach you what are the elements of the beginning of the oracles of God, and are become such as have need of milk, and not of solid food. For every one that partakes of milk is unskilled in the word of righteousness, for he is a babe; but solid food belongs to full-grown men, who, on account of habit, have their senses exercised for distinguishing both good and evil. Wherefore, leaving the word of the beginning of the Christ, let us go on to what belongs to full growth [perfection], not laying again a foundation of repentance from dead works and faith in God, of the doctrine of washings, and of imposition of hands, and of resurrection of the dead, and of eternal judgment; and this will we do if God permit. For it is impossible to renew again to repentance those once enlightened, and who have tasted of the heavenly gift, and have been made partakers of the Holy Spirit, and have tasted the good word of God, and the works of power of the age to come, and have fallen away, crucifying for themselves as they do the Son of God, and making a show of him. For ground which drinks the rain which comes often upon it, and produces useful herbs for those for whose sakes also it is tilled, partakes of blessing from God; but bringing forth thorns and briars, it is found worthless and nigh to a curse, whose end is to be burned. But we are persuaded concerning you, beloved, better things, and connected with salvation, even if we speak thus. For God is not unrighteous to forget your work, and the love which ye have shewn to his name, having ministered to the saints, and still ministering. But we desire earnestly that each one of you shew the same diligence to the full assurance of hope unto the end; that ye be not sluggish, but imitators of those who through faith and patience have been inheritors of the promises.

Shall we pray:

Dear heavenly Father, we do thank Thee for Thy precious Word. We just ask Thee to bless Thy

Word, breathe upon it by Thy Holy Spirit and make Thy Word living and operative to each one of us, and to Thee be all the glory. In the name of our Lord Jesus. Amen.

The book of Hebrews is a book of exhortation because in Hebrews 13:22 the writer tells us very clearly that he wrote this letter for the sake of exhortation. Exhortation in the Scripture means: "to call attention to, to encourage, and to warn against something."

There are altogether five distinctive exhortations in this letter of Hebrews. The first one is centered upon this matter of "so great salvation." The salvation that we have heard from our Lord Jesus, then from the apostles, and from those who receive from them is "so great salvation." It is not something small; it is great. It is so great that you cannot describe it; therefore, the author just says "so great salvation."

This salvation has to do not only with our sins forgiven, receiving eternal life, and going to heaven—as great as these are—but this "so great salvation" has something to do with glory. The only begotten Son of God came into this world to accomplish such a great salvation that He has now become the first born among many brethren, and He is to bring many sons, who are conformed to His image, into glory. Because this salvation is so great salvation we need to take heed abundantly to pay very close attention to what we have heard lest it slips away from us or we drift away from it through negligence, and we lose it.

Then we find the second exhortation is centered upon the "heavenly calling" that we have. We are called to be the house of God so that God may dwell among us; and what a holy house it must be! We are called to be the companions of Christ, the partakers of Christ, and we are called to enter into His rest that we may rest in His rest. This is our "heavenly calling" and because the calling is so heavenly we are encouraged to consider Him who is the great Apostle of our confession. Our Lord Jesus is the Apostle of our confession. God has sent Him into this world to accomplish such a great work and He has gone before as a forerunner into heaven itself. Therefore, we need to consider Him, to obey Him, to listen to Him, and to follow Him. We also need to encourage one another as long as it is today, because today is the day of salvation. We need to have a holy fear lest we miss it, lest we do not fulfill our calling, and we need to use diligence to enter into that rest.

The warning is: "... lest we have a wicked heart of unbelief." The heart is the most important thing. In our relationship with God if our heart is deceived by sin, then our heart can get so hardened that we cease to believe in God and what He can do for and in us, and because of this heart of unbelief, we may fall away from the living God.

Full Growth

The third exhortation we would like to consider is found in chapters 5, 6, and 7 of Hebrews. It is centered upon this matter of perfection. In chapter 6:1 it is said: "Wherefore, leaving the word of the beginning of the Christ, let us go on to what belongs to full growth."

In some versions it says: "... let us go on to perfection." Whether your version is "full growth" or "perfection," it is the same word in the original Greek. The word *perfection* means: "completeness, fulfillment, actual achievement of the end in view"; therefore, it means full growth or maturity.

Babes in Christ

Among God's people, roughly speaking, there are two different stages in our Christian life. One stage is babyhood and the other stage is manhood or womanhood. When we first believe in the Lord Jesus, we are babes in Christ. We are born again with a new life into the family of God. But even so, at that time we are just babes.

I think everybody loves a baby, but babyhood is just the first stage of life. It is beautiful within its time, but when it is time for a baby to grow up and outgrow babyhood into manhood or womanhood and it does not grow, then it becomes the ugliest thing in life. A life is born but that life is never able to arrive at its end; it is a waste instead of fulfilling its purpose. Therefore, after a baby is born we nourish that baby, we cherish it, and we help it to grow. One day when that baby grows into manhood or womanhood then the purpose of that life in that soul is fulfilled. The same thing is true in the spiritual realm. When we believe in the Lord Jesus, we are born again; we become babes in Christ.

MARKS OF BABYHOOD

Babies Need Milk

The first mark of babyhood is that a baby needs milk because he is not able to consume solid food. We know that milk is predigested food. A mother digests the food; it is then transformed into milk, and she is able to feed the baby. Babies cannot digest the food; therefore, somebody else has to do it for them and they receive the nutrition out of it. Spiritually, it means the beginning of the oracles of God or the beginning of the word of Christ. Milk nourishes us by giving us the knowledge of initial salvation. It tells us about Christ—His divinity, His humanity, that He is the Son of God who has become the Son of Man. It tells us how He died on the cross, bearing our sins upon Himself. It tells us how He was raised from the dead and is now in heaven. These are the beginnings of the word of Christ, the first elements of the gospel; and they are milk. We know that a baby can only consume milk because he is not ready to take in solid food.

Babies are Unskilled in the Word of Righteousness

The second mark of a baby is that he is not skilled in the word of righteousness. "For every one that partakes of milk is unskilled in the word of righteousness, for he is a babe" (Hebrews 5:13). In other words, what he knows is the word of grace. All he desires is grace—give me this and give me that. That is what a baby is crying out. He has no knowledge; he is unskilled in the word of righteousness. How can he be right? How should he live rightly before God? What should be his rightful relationship with God and with his brothers and sisters? He is not skilled in the word of righteousness. Not only is he not skilled, but he is scared of the word of righteousness because he thinks it is a hard word. It is too much for him; he is not ready for it.

Babes Are Fleshy

The third mark is found in I Corinthians 3:1: "And I, brethren, have not been able to speak to you as to spiritual but as to fleshly; as to babes in Christ." Sometimes this is translated "carnal," yet in the original there is a little variation. The word *fleshly* or *carnal* in the original is *sarkinos* which means "fleshy." That means the material you are made with. When you are a babe that is what you are—just flesh; that is what you are made of. But then in the 3rd verse it says, "Nor indeed are ye yet able; for ye are yet carnal." That word *carnal or sarkikos* is "fleshly." That means not only the material you are made of, but it is the moral condition that goes with it.

Dear brothers and sisters, when we are babes, we are fleshy. Will you forgive me if I say this? All the babies are so innocent, so beautiful, so lovely. But do you know that babes are all fleshy? It is all flesh—so self-centered. A baby never cares whether it is day or night; if he is hungry, he cries. It does not matter whether you are ready for him or not, he is ready and that is all that matters. He is fleshy; but even so, he is innocent, and that is the reason why we bear with him and love him. However, if that baby should never grow up according to the time he should be a man or she should be a woman, this is called fleshly in the Scriptures. There is a moral condition attached to it which is not very pleasing. So a babe in Christ is fleshy, but that is just for a period; it should not continue. If it continues long it becomes a serious problem. That is the reason why a child has to be disciplined. That fleshy has to be broken so that he or she may grow up into maturity.

Babes Walk According to the Natural Man

The fourth mark of a baby is that he acts and walks according to the natural man. Even though he is a believer, yet when he is in the baby stage, the way that he lives, the way he walks, even the way he talks is according to man. He is not very different from what the people around him are, and sometimes you wonder whether he is saved. He is saved, but he is still a baby. He has not grown up yet.

Babes Can Be Easily Swayed

Finally, the mark of a baby, as we find in Ephesians 4, is one who is easily tossed to and fro by every wind of doctrine according to the system of man. In other words, a baby can be easily swayed. When he hears one thing he falls for it; when he hears another thing he falls for it. He is changing all the time and there is not a stability that is established in his life. This shows that he is just a baby. He is exposed to every influence and every wind. When the wind blows this way, he goes this way; when the wind blows that way, he goes that way. These are the marks of babyhood.

MATURITY

It is the will of God that we should outgrow that babyhood and grow into perfection or maturity. Of course, there is a slight difference when we compare the physical and the spiritual. In the physical we begin as a babe, and if everything goes all right after twenty years we grow into manhood or womanhood. In China it is often said that a person has to wait until they are thirty years old before they are established.

Maybe in this country it is earlier, but there needs to be a certain time. After a certain number of years have passed it seems almost natural for a person to enter into maturity or full growth.

In the spiritual realm there is a little difference. It is true that years should mellow a person because we do need time to grow, but this is not proportionally true. In other words, someone can grow out of babyhood into manhood quicker than someone else. It is not like in the natural life where it has to be twenty or thirty years. Some people may grow faster; others may grow slower, and the reason has something to do with our heart condition and desire. If we desire to grow, if we seek for perfection, there is a chance for us to grow faster and earlier; but if we are dull and sluggish, we may be content to be a babe. Isn't that strange that we would be content to be a babe? I wonder if any baby is content to be a baby. I think the desire of babies is to grow and not remain as babes. How they long to grow up!

I have a younger sister, and one day, when she was only a few years old, she and my cousin of the same age were sitting on the stairway talking to each other. People overheard these two little girls complaining to each other that they were the youngest of the family. They were not happy about it because as they looked at their big sisters and brothers they wanted to be like them. They thought that by being so small they were in a disadvantaged position. They were not happy with it. Isn't that strange? Children like to grow but grown-ups like to become children. We do not want to grow; we want to remain as babes.

CHRIST AS PERFECTION

The word *perfection* in the New Testament does not speak of sinless perfect. There is only one Man in the whole world who is sinless perfect or perfection in the absolute sense, and that is the Lord Jesus. He is the only one that is sinless perfect. Nevertheless, even the Son, who is so perfect, had to learn obedience through the things which He suffered. After He had been perfected He became the Author of our eternal salvation (see Hebrews 5:8-9).

So far as the Lord Jesus is concerned, He was perfect in the absolute sense, and yet He had to learn obedience. As the Son of God, He is God; how can He know obedience? God is the authority; therefore, when the Lord Jesus came into this world, there was something He had to learn. He had to learn obedience to His heavenly Father, and He learned this through the things which He suffered. Thus, He was perfected to be the Author of our eternal salvation. In other words, He accomplished the goal. Through His obedience and through His suffering He was able to accomplish the work of redemption that He was sent for and thus became the Author of our eternal salvation.

CHRIST—OUR PERFECTION

This is about the Lord Jesus, but how about us? We are not sinless perfect. We never will be until we are unclothed with this old tabernacle and clothed with a new building—a spiritual body. Only then will we no longer sin. Therefore, according to the New Testament when perfection applies to believers, it means "maturity, growing up, full growth." We need to grow up; we need to mature. We should not remain as babes in Christ.

Growing up into maturity does not mean that after we have believed in the Lord Jesus for maybe three or five years and have grown in the knowledge of the Word or in the times of our fellowship together that we are mature. Thank God, we need to grow in the knowledge of the Word and in fellowship, but strictly speaking, growing up or maturity simply means that the life of Christ or the measure of Christ is increased within us. That is growth. In other words, it is not just a growth in our minds. After we believe in the Lord Jesus we may attend services every Sunday and hear many of man's sermons and messages so that our mind is stocked with teachings and doctrines, and somehow we think we have grown. No, that is not the meaning of growth here; it is not perfection.

Growth does not mean that we become very active in the church, although I think every member of the body of Christ needs to be active in the church. If a member is not active, sooner or later he will be paralyzed. Would you rather be a paralyzed member in the body of Christ or an active member of the body of Christ? To be an active member sometimes you have to be disciplined, that is true; but if you are paralyzed you are beyond discipline. However, even if you are an active member of the body of Christ and engaged in many so-called Christian activities, it does not mean you have grown. Not at all! The point is whether Christ has increased in you. When you believe in Him, you know Him as your Savior; but is your knowledge of Christ experiential or mental? Have you experienced Christ in an increasing, additional degree and more abundantly?

Paul said: "To know Him ..." Of course, we know that Paul already knew Him. He met Him on the road to Damascus and had served the Lord for many years. He was now in prison in Rome for the gospel's sake and yet his cry was still to know Him. "Oh, that I may know Him, to know the power of His resurrection, to have fellowship with His suffering, to be conformed to

His death, that I may arrive at the out-resurrection, select resurrection out of death" (see Philippians 3:10-11). This is full growth or maturity. May we continue to know Him, to grow in His life, that He may be formed in us and we may be fully conformed to His image. That is maturity. This is something that we must press on toward, and we must know.

Are we content with the little that we know of Christ? Thank God, the little we know, so far as it is concerned, is great because we know Jesus Christ as the Son of God, as Christ, and we know Him as our personal Savior. But if we are just content with the little that we know of Christ and refuse to press on to know and experience Him more, we will remain as babes and be a sorrow not only to God but also to ourselves. Some people do not want to grow because with growth there is responsibility. We want to be babes and let other people take the responsibility for us. We give them problems and let them bear the responsibilities. There are people like that among believers. They do not want to take any responsibility so they do not want to grow because with responsibility there has to be suffering. Suffering goes with responsibility, and they are afraid of suffering, afraid to pay the cost. Because of that they stay in babyhood.

What is the will of God for His people? The will of God for His people is that we may grow up into sonship. John 1:12 tells us that anyone who receives Him or believes in His name is given authority to become a child of God. When we believe in the Lord Jesus, we become little children of God, babes in Christ. Thank God for that. But what is the purpose of God in saving us? What is the purpose of God concerning us? He does not want just babies. He is not opening a nursery. He wants grown-up sons who are people that can share responsibility with Him. That is God's purpose. God's purpose concerning us is sonship.

In Galatians 4 we are told that in the fullness of time God sent His Son into this world, born of woman, born under the law, that He might deliver us from the curse of the law so that we may receive sonship. God wants us to be sons and daughters. He wants us to grow up. If this is

God's will for us, do we think we can sit back and say, "I am quite happy just to be a babe"? We may be happy now, but one day we will be sorrowful, not to say our heavenly Father is sorrowful. This is a very important thing before us. God's will is that we go on to full growth. He does not want any one of us to remain as babes.

How many years have you believed in the Lord? When Paul wrote to the Corinthians he had been in Corinth previously for a year and a half. He left them for a few years and wrote this first letter to them in which he said: "According to this time you should not be babes anymore. I should be able to share with you meat, but I am not able to because you are still carnal; you have not grown" (see 3:1-3).

We find the same thing in the letter to the Hebrews: "According to the time you should be teachers and able to teach others, but unfortunately you are still babes. You are not able to consume solid food; you are still looking for milk and nothing but milk" (see 5:12-14). Isn't that a sad thing? Are we so dull in our hearing, so sluggish? Have we become so lazy, so indifferent, so careless that we cease to grow? Do we know that the only safety for us is to press on? If we stay put, we will go backward. If we slow down, we not only stop but we go back. The only way for us is to go on.

FOUNDATION DOCTRINES

"Wherefore, leaving the word of the beginning of the Christ, let us go on to what belongs to full growth, [perfection]" (Hebrews 6:1). The exhortation is to press on. The "word of the beginning of the Christ" is the word of the foundation. In other words, these are foundation truths.

Repentance from Dead Works and Faith in God

"Not laying again a foundation of repentance from dead works and faith in God" (Hebrews 6:1b). The first set of the foundation truths is repentance from dead works and faith in God. It does not say repentance from sins; we all know we need to repent of our sins. But it says repent from dead works, and these are good works. When we first realize that we have sinned, we try to do some good works to cover up our sins or to substitute in some way for our sins or to redeem our sins. These are dead works because they are done by a dead man. They are good works but they come out of a dead man who is dead in sins and transgressions. Unless the Holy Spirit shows the need to repent of good works most people depend on that. They depend on their good works. When they realize that they have sinned, they try to depend on their good works to go to God, but one day the Holy Spirit will show them their works are dead. The dead works are utterly undependable, just like the fig leaves that Adam and Eve made to put on as an apron. They think this will cover their nakedness; but the wind blows. We need to repent from dead works. It is only when we repent from dead works that we have faith in God; in other words, we cease to believe in ourselves anymore. There is nothing to trust. We have believed in God and in what He has provided for us. It is the past. We have repented; we have believed.

The Doctrine of Washings and of Imposition of Hands

There are two foundation truths in the second set—the doctrine of washings and of imposition of hands. Notice it is not "washings"; it is the "doctrine of washings" or baptism. The teaching of baptism is union with Christ. We, who are baptized, are baptized unto Christ and into His death. We are identified with Christ in His death, burial and resurrection. So the teaching of baptism is union with Christ. Thank God for this union.

The teaching of the laying on of hands is the union of the body. In other words, through the laying on of hands we are identified with one another. That is why Ananias came to Paul, put his hand on him and said, "Brother, the Lord has sent me to pray for you that you might see." Ananias identified himself with Paul, and through the laying on of hands Paul was identified with Ananias into the body of Christ. This is the present. We are united with Christ and we are united with one another in the body of Christ.

Resurrection of the Dead and Eternal Judgment

The third set of the foundation truths is resurrection of the dead and of eternal judgment. In the future there will be the resurrection of the dead. Those who believe in the Lord Jesus will be resurrected from the dead, put on a spiritual body, and enter into life. Those who are not of the Lord will be resurrected a thousand years later, but they will appear before the great white throne and be judged unto eternal death. Hence, the resurrection of the dead and of eternal judgment concerns the future.

These three sets of teachings are the word of the beginning of Christ. This is the foundation truth, and we must have that foundation. If you do not have that foundation you are not the Lord's; you do not belong to the Lord. But if you have the foundation, then you belong to the Lord; you are the Lord's. Thank God, the foundation is already laid; but then what? The Bible says, "Leaving the word of the beginning of the Christ let us press on to perfection not laying again the foundation." This is not in contradiction to chapter 3:14 which says: "For we are become companions of the Christ if indeed we hold the beginning of the assurance firm to the end."

It says we have to "... hold the beginning firm to the end," and in chapter 6 it says, "Wherefore, leaving the word of the beginning of the Christ." Is there any contradiction? No. The beginning is the root out of which we grow, and we never leave it; it is always there. The foundation is always there. In other words, we do not leave the foundation. It is there and out of that we grow up. But so far as the beginning is just the commencement of something for the future, then we have to leave the commencement and go ahead. Otherwise, we are just circling around the foundation and we never move forward. We will be like the children of Israel. They were saved, delivered out of Egypt, and they were supposed to go into the Promised Land. But somehow they wandered around in circles in the wilderness and never outgrew it.

We have been saved for three, five or ten years—maybe more; where are we now? Have we grown in Christ? Or are we still in babyhood? Are these marks of babyhood still characterizing our lives? Or is Christ being formed in us that He may be seen and heard by other people, and we are now a blessing to other people?

Have we pressed on? Of course, we know that pressing on needs a little effort. If we do not exert any effort and just take it easy, we drift. We have to apply ourselves to God's calling; we have to set our heart upon Him. We have to desire to know Him; to be willing to suffer and pay the cost. Only when we press on, will there be full growth. It is not automatic—after twenty years we are automatically full grown—no! It depends on how we respond, how we desire Him, how we press on. Therefore, we need to leave the beginning behind, but that does not mean we leave the foundation because it is already there. However, if the foundation is not there, then we need to lay it; but if the foundation is already there, then there is no way to relay it.

"For it is impossible to renew again to repentance those once enlightened, and who have tasted of the heavenly gift, and have been made partakers of the Holy Spirit and have tasted the good Word of God, and the works of power of the age to come" (Hebrews 6:4,5).

"It is impossible to renew again ..." The word *renew* in the original means "entirely new." It is not just to remodel it or renovate it. It means to start all over again, make it entirely new, a fresh start.

"Those once enlightened ..." We have been enlightened through the Holy Spirit convicting us of our sins, and we have repented and believed in the Lord Jesus.

"Who have tasted of the heavenly gift ..." The heavenly gift is Christ who is the bread of life. He is our life—that is the heavenly gift, eternal life.

"Have been made partakers of the Holy Spirit ..." If we believe in the Lord Jesus the Holy Spirit dwells in us. We have been made partakers of the Holy Spirit.

"Have tasted the good Word of God ..." The word *tasted* here does not mean we have heard only. It does not mean that we only understand it in our mind. The word *tasted* means we have enjoyed it, we have experienced it, and it is very real and enjoyable. Now, we have enjoyed the Word of God. Thank God, we are saved. As a result of being saved, we love the Word of God, we enjoy it, we taste it—it is sweeter than the honeycomb. Then we have tasted the "works of power of the age to come." That is the power of the Holy Spirit and the gifts of the Holy Spirit that we have tasted.

Here you find a person who is soundly saved, the foundation is already laid. For such a person it is impossible to relay the foundation, because the foundation is already there.

"And have fallen away ..." Falling away means falling away from the goal. There is a goal and the goal is perfection or full growth. If we fall away from the goal and can relay the foundation (that means if we can re-repent as if we had never believed in the Lord Jesus), it will be like crucifying the Son of God the second time. It is impossible!

Once we are enlightened, once we have received the new life, once we have received the

Holy Spirit, once we have tasted the good Word of God, once we have the foundation in our life, we need to remember that this foundation can never be re-laid. It is there.

If we fall away from the goal of perfection, if we become dull and sluggish, if we stand back and do not grow, what happens? It is true, falling away is a serious thing. In I Corinthians 10 we are told if anyone "thinks that he stands take care lest he fall." It is the same word. The children of Israel fell and fell and fell until finally at Kadesh-Barnea they fell again and there was no point of return. But who are we to say to any one, "You are beyond repentance because you have fallen away and you are finished." No! The writer of the book of Hebrews says, "But we think better things about you. Even though I am talking this way you are better than that. You have not fallen away to the point of no return; that is apostasy. You have fallen away because you have become dull, you have become sluggish, and you are not diligent. That is why you have fallen away."

Therefore, if that is the reason and we realize that we have fallen away, we cannot go back to the very beginning before we were saved and be saved again and relay the foundation. Then what do we do? Just get up and go ahead.

Suppose I am walking to this place from my home and midway I fall. Do I roll back to my home, get up and start walking again? Nonsense! If I fall down, I get up and walk forward until I arrive there. This is what the Scripture is trying to tell us. Suppose there is one who has fallen away. This person cannot start from the very beginning because the foundation is already there. There is no way to do it again. Just get up and go on.

"For ground which drinks the rain which comes often upon it, and produces useful herbs for those for whose sakes also it is tilled, partakes of blessing from God; but bringing forth thorns and briars, it is found worthless and nigh to a curse, whose end is to be burned" (Hebrews 6:7,8).

It is like ground that receives rain from above. The seed is already there and when the rain comes upon it, it should bring forth herbs for those who till it—that is, for God. God has put the seed in us, His life in us, and He is raining His blessing from above upon us in order that we may produce fruit for His pleasure. But if we do not produce the herbs for His purpose and instead waste all the blessings of God in our lives, we will produce thorns and briars.

What are thorns and briars? We are told that thorns are aborted fruit. In other words, instead of bearing fruit for God we live according to the flesh. We just want to do what we want to do; we do not care about God. If we go on like that, we waste the grace of God and will only produce thorns and briars. Then we become worthless to God and nigh to a curse. Underline the word *nigh*. It is not a curse, but *nigh* to a curse—very close—whose end is to be burned.

What does it mean to be burned? Thorns and briars are burned, but the ground cannot be burned. In other words, the foundation is Christ and He can never be burned, but what you build upon that foundation will all be burned. This is I Corinthians chapter 3. But thank God that the writer says, "We are persuaded concerning you, beloved, better things" (6:9a). In other words, you are better than that. You are not that bad yet; you are very hopeful. So take heart and if we have become dull in hearing, if we have become sluggish, if our hearts have become hardened, if we have fallen away, may the Spirit of God speak to us and get us up and push us on to perfection. There is still time for it. We do not have much more time, but there is still time. I often thank God for today because as long as there is today there is opportunity. Let us press on to perfection.

"But we desire earnestly that each one of you shew the same diligence to the full assurance of hope unto the end; that ye be not sluggish, but imitators of those who through faith and patience have been inheritors of the promises" (6:11-12).

What is perfection? Perfection or full growth is to inherit the promises of God—not just to inherit one promise but to inherit all the promises of God. In other words, in this section of the book of Hebrews we find what we need to consider is Jesus as the High Priest of our confession. In the second exhortation we need to consider Christ as the Apostle of our confession because it is connected with calling but in this matter of perfection we need to consider Jesus as the High Priest of our confession. He is our High Priest, not according to the order of Aaron, but after the order of Melchisedec.

Dear brothers and sisters, to know Christ as our Savior is milk; to know Christ as our High Priest after the order of Melchisedec is solid food. How can we grow unless we know Him as our High Priest? When Abraham came back from the battle, Melchisedec, the high priest, met him, gave him bread and wine, and blessed him. This is a picture of Christ our High Priest after the order of Melchisedec. We have received His life in us, but how can we live a heavenly life upon this earth? Where does the power come from for living a heavenly life? Where does the power come from for overcoming temptations? Where does the power come from for reaching the goal that God has set before us, unless we know Him as our High Priest? He is our High Priest.

Christ is the Mediator of the New Covenant. In other words, God has given us the New Covenant in which are all the promises of God. Christ as our High Priest is to mediate the New Covenant; that is to say, He is to bring the blessings of the New Covenant to us, and that is why He intercedes daily for us as He is seated at the right hand of the Father. As He intercedes the Holy Spirit, who is in us, begins to work in every one of us to bring us into all the fullness of the promises of God that we may inherit what God has promised. If we do not depend upon Christ as our High Priest, who are we depending upon for daily life? We depend on ourselves. We try to live a Christian life, a victorious life, a heavenly life, but we discover that we are bound to earth; we cannot do it. But thank God, if we depend on Him who is now at the right hand of God making intercession for us, then through the supply of the Holy Spirit we will be able to experience the power of that heavenly life and inherit all the promises of God. This is the secret to perfection.

May I put it this way? Without Christ as our High Priest, perfection is impossible, but with

Christ as our High Priest perfection is ours. The promises of God do not automatically come upon us. Just because God has a promise, therefore we automatically inherit it. No. All the promises of God depend on our response to the working of the Holy Spirit. When the Holy Spirit works in us, we respond with faith and patience, and then we may have it. But if we do not respond with faith and instead we are impatient, we do not inherit it. That is why in the last part of chapter 6 the example is given of Abraham who inherited the promise of God because he believed and he was patient.

Dear brothers and sisters, thank God for all the promises. Through all the precious promises of God we may grow into sonship. The promises are given to us that we may live a godly life and enter into perfection. But how are we to inherit all these promises? We must believe. When the Holy Spirit brings God's promise to our attention, believe it; and not only believe it, but patiently wait for it. God called Abraham out of Ur of Chaldea and gave him a promise. He waited patiently, believing until he got the promise. So may the Lord help us.

Let us conclude by saying that perfection, full-growth, or sonship is God's purpose for every child of God. This is what we need to aim at. Never become contented to remain as babes in Christ. Press on to perfection. Do not be sluggish and dumb. May we be diligent knowing Christ as our High Priest after the order of Melchisedec, which means after the power of an indissoluble life. It is by faith and patience that we inherit the promise like our father of belief, Abraham. So may the Lord help us.

Shall we pray:

Dear heavenly Father, do impress upon our hearts that it is Thy will for us to grow into perfection. Do not allow us to remain as babes, but Lord, we pray that Thou wilt create such a longing for Thyself that we may press on to know Thee unto full growth. And our Father, we do acknowledge that by ourselves we cannot make it but we know that Thy Son, our Lord Jesus Christ, is now seated at Thy right hand as our High Priest, interceding for us that He may save us to the uttermost. So Father, we just ask Thee to open our eyes to see Christ as our High Priest that we may daily depend on Him, and through the working of the Holy Spirit, by faith and patience, inherit the inheritance. We ask in the name of our Lord Jesus. Amen.

LIFE IN THE HOLIEST

Hebrews 10:19-31: Having therefore, brethren, boldness for entering into the holy of holies by the blood of Jesus, the new and living way which he has dedicated for us through the veil, that is, his flesh, and having a great priest over the house of God, let us approach with a true heart, in full assurance of faith, sprinkled as to our hearts from a wicked conscience, and washed as to our body with pure water. Let us hold fast the confession of the hope unwavering, (for he is faithful who has promised;) and let us consider one another for provoking to love and good works; not forsaking the assembling of ourselves together, as the custom is with some; but encouraging one another, and by so much the more as ye see the day drawing near. For where we sin willfully after receiving the knowledge of the truth, there no longer remains any sacrifice for sins, but a certain fearful expectation of judgment, and heat of fire about to devour the adversaries. Any one that has disregarded Moses' law dies without mercy on the testimony of two or three witnesses: of how much worse punishment, think ye, shall he be judged worthy who has trodden under foot the Son of God, and esteemed the blood of the covenant, whereby he has been sanctified, common, and has insulted the Spirit of grace? For we know him that said, To me belongs vengeance; I will recompense, saith the Lord: and again, The Lord shall judge his people. It is a fearful thing falling into the hands of the living God.

Let us pray:

Dear heavenly Father, we do thank Thee for Thy precious Word. We ask, Lord, that Thou wilt breathe upon Thy Word and make it living to us. We pray that as we go into Thy Word we may hear Thy voice speaking to us directly, and to Thee be all the glory. In the name of our Lord Jesus. Amen.

The book of Hebrews is a book of exhortation. It is written as a letter of exhortation (see Hebrews 13:22). In this letter to the Hebrews, we find five distinctive exhortations and each one is centered upon some important theme. Because of the importance of what the author is presenting to us, he encourages us on the one hand and warns us on the other.

We would like to enter into the fourth exhortation which is found in chapters 8—10. In chapter 10 we read these words: "Having therefore, brethren ..." "Therefore" is a word that shows us there is a continuation of what has already been said. If we read from chapter 8 through chapter 10, we will find a number of things there. These things are there for the sake of enabling us to enter into the holy of holies.

I wonder how much we understand about this matter of entering into the holy of holies. The holy of holies, or the holiest, is actually the place where the glory of God abides. Entering into the holy of holies means to enter into the very presence of God, to live in the very presence of God, to behold His face, to commune with Him, to have fellowship with Him, to abide in Him.

This is a privilege that people did not have in the Old Testament time because they had to worship God from far away.

In the Old Testament God wanted to dwell among His people and to do that He commanded Moses to build Him a tabernacle. The tabernacle has an outer court, a holy place, and the holy of holies. The people could enter into the outer court to offer sacrifices to God, but they were not allowed to enter into the holy place. Only a few people, the priesthood, could enter into the holy place to serve God, but they were not allowed to enter into the holy of holies. Only the high priest, one man in all the nation of Israel, was allowed to enter into the holy of holies once a year. He went behind the veil, for a little while, with blood and smoke of incense to cover him, to offer blood atonement for the whole nation. According to the interpretation of the Holy Spirit in Hebrews, it simply means the way to the holiest had not been opened. In other words, no one could see the face of God. No one could enter into His presence, not to say, live in His presence. That was a privilege never granted in the Old Testament time; but thank God, today we are able to enter into the holy of holies.

As you read chapter 8 you find under the Old Covenant of law the Ten Commandments: "thou shall" and "thou shall not." These are the demands of God; yet no one can fulfill such demands. Under the law everyone was condemned. But thank God, He has covenanted with us with a New Covenant, a covenant of grace. In other words, it is no longer "thou shall" and "thou shall not," putting all the responsibility on man. It is, "I will" and "I will." It is a covenant of grace. God says: I will do everything for you. I will forgive your sins, and I will forget your iniquities. I will dwell in you. I will give you the spirit of wisdom and revelation that you may know Me. I will give you My own life that you may have the power to obey Me. In other words, God promised He would do everything for us and this has been sealed by the blood of our Lord Jesus. It is a covenant that cannot be broken.

In the Old Covenant the responsibility was upon man, and when man failed to fulfill his responsibility God abolished the covenant because it did not work. But in the New Covenant God put all the responsibility upon Himself and thank God He never fails. Therefore this covenant can never be broken. Under the New Covenant of grace we can enter into the holy of holies.

In chapter 9 we find that under the Old Covenant there were sacrifices made because without the shedding of blood there is no remission of sins. That is the reason why the children of Israel had to offer sacrifices again and again, day after day, month after month, year after year. But the Bible tells us the blood of bulls and goats really cannot wash our sins away. In other words, they serve as a type, as a shadow. The blood of the bulls and the goats only covers, as it were, our sins before God for a time. The next year the blood of bulls and goats had to be offered and brought within the veil to make atonement before God again. The sins had not been forgiven; they were just covered for a time. Until one day the blood of our Lord Jesus, who offered Himself by the eternal Spirit, spotless to God, cleansed us from all our sins once and for all.

Dear brothers and sisters, it is the blood of the Lord Jesus that washed all our sins away forever. Once and for all it is finished. In the Old Testament time there were many sacrifices; but here in the New Testament, through the offering of our Lord Jesus it is just once, and it is perfected. He has perfected eternal redemption for us.

Under the Old Covenant you needed priests—human beings such as we. They were weak too, but they were priests according to the Levitical order. They helped the people to offer sacrifices. However, the priesthood often was interrupted by death. In the New Covenant we have a priest, Jesus Christ. He is after the order of Melchizedek. In other words, after the like order of the indissoluble life, He lives forever making intercession for us that He may save us to the uttermost.

In the Old Testament times the high priest entered into the holy of holies once a year with the blood of the sacrifice, but now the shadow has passed away. We have the reality now because the Lord Jesus has taken His own blood, not into a man-made tent, but into heaven itself. The time of shadow is past. Now Christ has brought us into reality. Today, we are able not only to enter into the very presence of God, but by His grace we are able to dwell in His presence. Dear brothers and sisters, this is the highest privilege that man can ever enjoy, and thank God it is ours.

The Way into the Holy of Holies

The writer of the Hebrews says that we may approach and enter into the holy of holies with boldness. Now we can draw near to the very presence of God, no longer with fear and trembling far, far away, but with holy boldness. This boldness is not based upon ourselves. If it were based upon ourselves it would be presumptuous. In the Old Testament times, at the very beginning, two priests, who were sons of Aaron, presumptuously tried to enter into the tent of meeting to offer incense to God with strange fire, and they were burned to death. So it is not by any boldness in ourselves because in ourselves there is no good. We are not worthy. We could not stand under that impenetrable light. We cannot stand the light of God, the holiness of God. But thank God, our boldness is in Christ Jesus.

Here you find we have the boldness to enter into the holy of holies by three things. The first one is by the blood of the Lamb. We are able to enter into the very presence of God and stand before Him with boldness because the blood of the Lord Jesus has been shed. His blood has washed all our sins away so when we stand before God, God can see no iniquity in us. It is all washed away by the blood of our Lord Jesus and that is where our boldness is.

Secondly, the Lord Jesus has opened for us a new and living way through the veil—His own flesh. When our Lord Jesus was crucified on Calvary's cross, at the moment He died something happened in the city of Jerusalem in the temple. There the veil that separated the holiest of all from the holy place was rent from top to bottom into two. Through the breaking of the body of our Lord Jesus on Calvary's cross, the veil that stood between the holiest of all and the holy place was rent in two. The way to the presence of God was opened, and this is through the broken body of our Lord Jesus. He was broken on Calvary's cross to open the new and living way for all of us to enter in and to live in the presence of God.

The third thing is that today we have Him, our Lord Jesus, as our high priest of the house of God. He is now seated at the right hand of God making intercession for us, praying for us, supplying us with His own life, with His Spirit, with His power, that we may live a life that will be pleasing to God.

How we do thank God that through the blood and broken body of our Lord Jesus, and Him living forever for us as our High Priest, we have the boldness to enter into the holy of holies. Today, it is a reality that we cannot only enter in, but live there. We do not need to enter in and in a few minutes withdraw. No! We can live, dwell, abide, make our home in God, in His very presence and have loving fellowship with Him day by day, moment by moment. This is what the

Lord has done for us. Dear brothers and sisters, isn't this a marvelous privilege?

Today, we do not need to worship God from afar. We do not need to be in fear and trembling when we think about God. Today, we can come to God, dwell in Him, hold fellowship with Him, love Him, worship Him, gaze upon Him and be transformed by the Spirit of God that we may be conformed to the image of Christ. This is our portion, our privilege.

Now seeing such a tremendous privilege, the writer of Hebrews encourages us to approach. Why do we stay out? It cannot be imagined that we would stay away from Him when we have such a privilege as to be able to live daily in His presence, holding communion with Him, in sweet fellowship with Him. So the writer encourages us to approach: "Let us approach;" let us draw near.

A True Heart

"Let us draw near with a true heart." Brothers and sisters, it is a matter of heart; it is not a matter of outward appearance. The Lord

Jesus said: “The hour has come and now is that you do not worship God either at Mount Gerizim or in the temple in Jerusalem because you worship God in spirit and in truth” (see John 4:21). In other words, today it is not a matter of outward appearance, such as where or how. No, it is a matter of heart. Today we can approach God with a true heart because it has been sprinkled by the blood from an evil conscience. Formerly, there was an evil conscience in our heart. Whenever we thought of God our conscience would accuse us and we would flee from Him; we were afraid of Him. But thank God, our conscience has been cleansed and we have a conscience without offense before God. Today, we can approach God with a pure heart, with a true heart, with a heart that really desires God and loves God. We can approach God with our heart in full assurance of faith.

FAITH

This life within the veil, this life in the holiest of all, this life with God, in the presence of God, actually is a life of faith, of hope and of love. “Let us approach with a true heart, in full assurance of faith" (Hebrews 10:22).

We need to add a little strength to that translation because according to the original it is not the full assurance of faith, but it is the fullness of faith. Now there is a vast difference between full assurance of faith and fullness of faith. The fullness of faith means all that God has done in Christ objectively for us, and all that we trust and believe subjectively that He has done for us. In other words fullness of faith means: whatever the Lord has done for us, we believe and we appropriate. That is fullness of faith. We find this in Hebrews 11:1: "Now faith is the substantiating of things hoped for, the conviction of things not seen."

What is faith? "Faith is the substantiating of things hoped for." In other words, faith looks forward. It is something that we hope for; but even if it is something that we hope for, it is being brought to us now by faith. So it is called the substantiating of things hoped for.

Let me use an illustration. Here is a beautiful picture hanging on the wall. How is it that it becomes something that you can enjoy personally? The picture is a substance and when you see that picture your eyes substantiate it within you. Your eyes bring that beautiful scenery into your mind and because it is brought into your mind it gives you such enjoyment. That is what faith is. Faith substantiates all the promises of God. Faith brings all the things that Christ has done for us into our very life and makes them our experience so that we can enjoy them.

What is the life within the veil? The life in the presence of God is not a life by sight; it is a life by faith. If you live a life by sight, you live externally; you live by the circumstances around you, and what you see around you. As a matter of fact, what you see around you today will not give you much enjoyment. It is a sad sight. If you live by sight you are outside the veil. But dear brothers and sisters, we do not live by sight. We are to live by faith and we can live by faith because we see Him. We do not see other things—we see HIM. May I put it another way? We see all things through Him, and that makes all the difference. A life in the presence of God is a life of faith. It is a life that sees God continuously, looking off unto Jesus, the Author and Finisher of our faith. The more we look at Him, the more our faith increases and the more we are able to appropriate all that God has done for us in Christ Jesus. It is a life of faith.

HOPE

"Let us hold fast the confession of the hope unwavering, for he is faithful who has promised" (Hebrews 10:22). Secondly, this life in the presence of God is a life of hope. Robert Govett makes a distinction between profession and confession. Profession is made among people who are friendly. Confession renders in the presence of the enemy. In other words, confession is when you confess something, you acknowledge something, you declare something among people who are not friendly. That is confession, and it is "the confession of hope unwavering."

The world does not have hope. They have no hope, no God (see Ephesians 2). But we have a blessed hope, and what is the confession of hope that we have? "Christ in you, the hope of glory."

Our hope is that we may gain Him; we may know Him; we may know the power of His resurrection; we may be conformed to His death and arrive at the out-resurrection from among the dead; that we may be apprehended as we are being apprehended. Dear brothers and sisters, we have tremendous hope before us. *We have the hope to be transformed and conformed according to His image. We have the hope to rule and reign with Christ. We have the hope to be joined with Him eternally. We have the hope to be one with Him.* We have tremendous hope before Him and this is the hope that we confess, even today in this world.

It is true we have to hold fast the confession of our hope unwavering because we are surrounded by adverse situations. The whole world, everything around us is trying to destroy our hope, is trying to shake our hope. But thank God, we shall hold fast the confession of our hope unwavering because our God is faithful. We know that He will bring us to the end.

We are on an obstacle course; our life is such a big obstacle course. There are so many obstacles we have to overcome; but let us run with patience, laying aside every weight and the sin that easily entangles us, looking off unto Jesus, knowing that He has already run that race and He has won. Even if we have to suffer a little bit for it, it is worth it. And do not forget that God in His wisdom is child-training us that we may be made partakers of His divine nature (see Hebrews 12). Think of that blessed hope that is before us—a life in the presence of God is a life of hope.

Love

"And let us consider one another for provoking to love and good works" (Hebrews 10:24). A life in God is also a life of love, not only in the sense of loving God, but also loving one another. In Hebrews 13 it tells us that we need to be hospitable to one another, to remember those who are in bonds, to submit ourselves to the leaders and to go outside of the camp to join with Christ. It is a life of love.

These are the things we are encouraged to do. We are to approach, draw near to God and live this life of faith, of hope, and of love. Because of the greatness of the privilege, it brings to us also a tremendous responsibility. If we fail in our responsibility then of course we are warned that there will be a serious disciplinary action waiting for us. So the writer of the Hebrews not only encourages us to approach with a pure heart in fullness of faith, confession of hope, provoking to love and good works, but immediately he begins to warn us. Knowing that we have such a privilege, if we abuse the grace of God, if we despise the grace of God, what will happen?

WARNING

"For where we sin willfully after receiving the knowledge of the truth, there no longer remains any sacrifice for sins, but a certain fearful expectation of judgment, and heat of fire about to devour the adversaries" (Hebrews 10:26, 27)

Sometimes people say that Hebrews 10:26-31 refers to unbelievers. Whenever we read something that becomes serious, we think that it refers to other people. But if you read very carefully the context, you will find the writer to the Hebrews is not talking to unbelievers; he is talking to believers. He says, "For where we sin willfully..." The "we" is not only the Hebrews who received the letter, but even the writer of the book of Hebrews.

"After receiving the knowledge of the truth ..." The word "knowledge" in Greek is *epignosis* which is full knowledge, experiential knowledge. It is not just surface, mental knowledge. It is an experiential knowledge. In other words, you have already experienced the truth. "Having received the full knowledge of truth ..." An unbeliever doesn't have such knowledge—it is a believer.

"Of how much worse punishment, think ye, shall he be judged worthy who has trodden under foot the Son of God, and esteemed the blood of the covenant, whereby he has been sanctified, common, and has insulted the Spirit of grace?" (Hebrews 10:29)

In other words, he has been sanctified by the blood of the covenant. He was forgiven, his sins were washed away, he had that experience of what we call salvation and he has been sanctified by the covenant of the blood.

"The Lord shall judge His people" (verse 30b). We are His people. So these words are not spoken to unbelievers; they are spoken to believers. Oh brothers and sisters, because we have such high privilege, therefore we need to be severely warned, lest we abuse the grace of God and we despise what Christ has done for us.

"If we sin willfully ..." This word *willfully* means "deliberate, determined, sustained, continued." If we sin deliberately, decidedly, determinedly and continuously after we have known the Lord, after we are saved, after we know the truth, after we are sanctified then it is a serious thing. Now of course, the sin does not refer to the times when through temptation we fall. It does not refer to that. It does not refer to some sin that often entangles you. In other words, there may be some sin in your life you are fighting against all the time and yet you fail again and again. It does not refer even to that. It only refers to having received the full knowledge of God and yet sinning willfully against Him.

That is the sin that is mentioned there. If you read on, you will find it is described a little bit in verse 29: "Think ye, shall he be judged worthy who has trodden under foot the Son of God, and esteemed the blood of the covenant, whereby he has been sanctified, common?"

Apostasy

He has known the Son of God and yet he begins to tread the Son of God under his feet. He has been sanctified by the blood which is holy, yet he turns around and says it is common, it is nothing. He also insults the Spirit of grace. The Holy Spirit has wrought in his life and brings grace to him; yet he insults the Spirit of grace and despises the Spirit of God.

What is it? It is apostasy. In the Bible you will find there is warning against apostasy because apostasy is a possibility (see II Peter and Jude). In other words, people may have come to the knowledge of the Lord Jesus and then turn around completely and against Him in such a way that it is blasphemous. They misuse the grace of God for a dissolute life and they even deny their only Master and Lord, Jesus Christ. In history you find such cases, but thank God, not too many. Apostasy is possible; so we are warned against it. If such things should happen it says: "There no longer remains any sacrifice for sins, but a certain fearful expectation of judgment, and heat of fire about to devour the adversaries" (v. 27).

The writer used a comparison. He said if you disregard the Law of Moses, on the testimony of two or three you will die without mercy. That is true, because in the Old Testament when a person sinned and he knew about it, he could bring a sacrifice to God, ask for forgiveness and his sin would be covered. But there were certain sins people committed in the Old Testament under the Law of Moses that could not be sacrificed for. For instance, murder: Leviticus 21:12-14. If a person should kill another person deliberately there was no sacrifice for him, even if he should flee to the city of refuge. He had to be taken out and stoned to death—adultery: Deuteronomy 22:22. There were certain sins that were done deliberately against the law of Moses. And on the testimony of two or three these would be punished with death. Now if this is true in the Old Testament times how much more severe it will be in the New Testament times under grace with such tremendous privilege. When people turn around and trample Christ, the Son of God, under their feet, how much more severe the punishment will be. In other words, it is even more serious than death.

Thank God, those who believe in the Lord Jesus and have their sins forgiven and have received eternal life, God will never go back and take away eternal life. God will never again throw him into the lake of fire as if he has never believed because the calling and the gift of God knows no repentance. That is true but it is equally true that although God does not take away the eternal life, the gift He has given to us for eternity, if we willfully sin and do not repent, a severe disciplinary action is waiting for us. What is described there is fearful expectation of judgment. As a matter of matter of fact, that judgment is grace. Through judgment God will correct us, discipline us.

David's Sin

Let me use David as an illustration. David committed adultery and murder. After he committed that sin, God sent the prophet Nathan to him to point out to him what he had done. David was a man after God's own heart and his conscience had smitten him all the time, even before the prophet pointed it out. In other words, David really repented of what he had done and God told Nathan that He had forgiven him. But do you think he got off that easily? No!

"For thou desirest not sacrifice; else would I give it; thou hast no pleasure in burnt offering" (Psalm 51:16). David knew there was no sacrifice of sins for the sin of murder and adultery. David would have offered a sacrifice if God had desired it, but David knew it was no use; there was no sacrifice for sin. But does it mean there is nothing that can be done? Thank God, even though there remains no sacrifice for sin, yet David said the sacrifices of God are a broken spirit; "a broken and a contrite heart O God thou will not despise." David offered the sacrifices of a broken spirit, a contrite and broken heart and because of this God did not despise him. God said: “I will forgive you, but discipline and judgment will follow you and your house. You find that terrible things happened to David's house. He was forgiven, and yet severely punished, severely disciplined. It is the grace of God.

The sin of apostasy is a most serious sin. We do not know who has gone to the point of no return. We only hope that even though some have apostatized they will still repent and come to God with a broken and contrite heart. They will still be forgiven even though they have to be severely disciplined. But it is possible that in this life some people may go to the point of no return and if that is the case, then in the age to come they will be severely disciplined.

F. W. Newman

A very famous case on this matter of apostasy happened at the turn of the century. There was a very brilliant man by the name of F. W. Newman, Cardinal Newman's brother. He was a brilliant man and in his early days he was in constant company with great men of God such as J. N. Darby and Anthony Groves. He was really saved and seemed to love the Lord, but then at a certain period of his life he suddenly completely changed. For twenty years or so he became a skeptic. He began to oppose the truth of God and he polluted and deceived many young people in the university. He became an apostate. But thank God, before he died he repented and he asked that it be written on his tombstone that he died trusting in the blood of the Lord Jesus. So we feel that even though it is such a serious thing, yet God is so merciful that there is still opportunity for such people to return. The writer of the book of Hebrews goes on in verses 32-39: "But call to mind the earlier days in which, having been enlightened, ye endured much conflict of sufferings; on the one hand, when ye were made a spectacle both in reproaches and afflictions; and on the other, when ye became partakers with those who were passing through them. For ye both sympathized with prisoners and accepted with joy the plunder of your goods, knowing that ye have for yourselves a better substance, and an abiding one. Cast not away therefore your confidence, which has great recompense. For ye have need of endurance in order that, having done the will of God, ye may receive the promise. For yet a very little while he that comes will come, and will not delay. But the just shall live by faith; and, if he draw back, my soul does not take pleasure in him. But we are not drawers back to perdition, but of faith to saving the soul."

This is a real comfort. Even though we find the warning is so serious, yet we do not need to be afraid. By the grace of God He has supported us and supplied us that we may continue on, enduring with faith and not drawing back. Brothers and sisters, just a little while, it will not be long. Even though it is difficult, it is just a little while and He that comes will come and the just shall live by faith. So may the Lord help us.

Shall we pray:

Dear heavenly Father, we do praise and thank Thee that Thou hast given us such high privilege, privilege that people in the old days could never have, but thank God it is our portion that we may dwell in Thy very presence and have sweet communion with Thee daily. Our Father, we pray that having such privilege through the blood of the Lamb and the new and living way Christ has opened for us with Him as our High Priest, that we may draw near with boldness, with a true heart with fullness of faith and hope unwavering, and provoking one another to love and good works as long as it is today. Lord, we pray that this may be true with all of us. Do deliver us from willfully sinning against Thee and turning our back against Thee. We cannot keep ourselves, but we commit ourselves to Thee knowing that Thou art able to keep us until that day, and to Thee be all the praise and glory. In the name of our Lord Jesus. Amen.

THE PRIZE

Hebrews 12:12-29—Wherefore lift up the hands that hang down, and the failing knees; and make straight paths for your feet, that that which is lame be not turned aside; but that rather it may be healed. Pursue peace with all, and holiness, without which no one shall see the Lord: watching lest there be any one who lacks the grace of God; lest any root of bitterness springing up trouble you, and many be defiled by it; lest there be any fornicator, or profane person, as Esau, who for one meal sold his birthright; for ye know that also afterwards, desiring to inherit the blessing, he was rejected, for he found no place for repentance although he sought it earnestly with tears. For ye have not come to the mount that might be touched and was all on fire, and to obscurity, and darkness, and tempest, and trumpet's sound, and voice of words; which they that heard, excusing themselves, declined the word being addressed to them any more: for they were not able to bear what was enjoined. And if a beast should touch the mountain, it shall be stoned; and, so fearful was the sight, Moses said, I am exceedingly afraid and full of trembling; but ye have come to mount Zion; and to the city of the living God, heavenly Jerusalem; and to myriads of angels, the universal gathering; and to the assembly of the firstborn who are registered in heaven; and to God, judge of all; and to the spirits of just men made perfect; and to Jesus, mediator of a new covenant; and to the blood of sprinkling, speaking better than Abel. See that ye refuse not him that speaks. For if those did not escape who had refused him who uttered the oracles on earth, much more we who turn away from him who does so from heaven: whose voice then shook the earth; but now he has promised, saying, Yet once will I shake not only the earth, but also the heaven. But this Yet once, signifies the removing of what is shaken, as being made, that what is not shaken may remain. Wherefore let us, receiving a kingdom not to be shaken, have grace, by which let us serve God acceptably with reverence and fear. For also our God is a consuming fire.

Let us pray:

Dear heavenly Father, as we are before Thy Word we pray that we may be those who tremble at Thy Word and obey Thy voice. We do commit this time into Thy hands and ask Thee to encourage, warn and exhort us. In the name of our Lord Jesus. Amen.

The fifth exhortation that we find in the book of Hebrews is found in chapters 11—13 and it is centered upon the goal, the prize of the calling on high. It is centered upon the better, the heavenly country, the holy city, the New Jerusalem. It is centered upon the birthright and the blessing of the firstborn. It is centered upon the kingdom, the kingdom that cannot be shaken. We find all these as the goal that is set before us and because of such a goal we are encouraged and we are also warned.

The Arena of Faith

Chapter 11 of Hebrews is a chapter on faith. Sometimes we call this chapter the arena of faith and it is as if the Holy Spirit has put us into that arena and lets us view these men and women of faith. The faith of these men and women, as we find in chapter 11, can be summed up in this verse: "But without faith it is impossible to please [God]. For he that draws near to God must believe that he is, and that he is a rewarder of them who seek him out" (Hebrews 11:6).

Without faith it is impossible to please God. This is how important faith is, and the faith mentioned in this chapter is the faith that: "he who draws near to God must believe that God is." It is not in the sense of believing there is God because we have already believed that there is God. We have already believed in God, but the faith here is that we believe God is; we believe that God is the great I AM. We believe He is the I AM as we find in the Gospel according to John, and we also believe that He is a rewarder of him who seeks Him out.

This is not the initial faith, but this is the more advanced faith. The initial faith is when we begin to believe in the Lord Jesus as our personal Savior. We need to have that faith, but it is supposed that we already have it. So here it is the more advanced faith. We not only believe that our Lord Jesus, the Son of God, is our Christ, is our Savior, but we also believe that He is the great I AM, and we believe that if we seek Him we will be rewarded. In other words, it is not a matter of gift; it is a matter of reward. If we believe in the Lord Jesus as our Savior, we receive the gift of eternal life. After we believe in the Lord Jesus and we believe that He is the great I AM, He is what He is, He is all that He is to us, He is everything to us, then we will be rewarded.

These men and women mentioned in this chapter in the arena of faith have all received revelation from above, because without revelation there can be no faith. When God revealed Himself to these men and women they responded with faith and through faith they turned their vision into vocation. All of them have achieved something, the achievement of faith, and they have all been given testimony by God that God was pleased with them. However, in spite of the fact that these men and women have all achieved something for God by faith and they all received testimony from above, yet the Bible says they have not received the promise.

The Promise

"And these all, having obtained witness through faith, did not receive the promise" (Hebrews 11:39). What is the promise? These men and women have received lots of things. They even received testimony from God that they had pleased Him, and yet the Spirit of God said they did not receive the promise. Why? Because they could not.

"God having foreseen some better thing for us, that they should not be made perfect without us" (Hebrews 11:40). In other words, this promise must be something corporate. It is not something personal. It is a corporate promise and it cannot be fulfilled individually. It has to be fulfilled together—these men and women of faith together with us.

The promise that is spoken of here is the same promise that Abraham, Isaac, and Jacob all looked forward to. By faith Abraham left his native place. He obeyed God and followed God to the place that was promised to him, but during his lifetime he never actually received the Promised Land. He only bought a cave and adjoining field for burial. Yet the Bible says he was actually looking for something far more than Canaan. God promised him Canaan, that's true, but through Canaan he saw *the* promise and the promise is the heavenly country. If he thought of his old country he could go back if he wanted to, but he refused to go back. He would rather be a stranger and sojourner on earth because he was looking for a better country, a heavenly country, a city with foundations which God is building.

This city with foundations is the holy city, the New Jerusalem. In Revelation 21 and 22 you find this city, which God has built, has twelve foundations, and this is what these men and women are looking forward to. And dear brothers and sisters, in a sense, this is what we are looking forward to.

Thank God, we have an eternal home, a place where God is all and in all because in that holy city, the New Jerusalem, the glory of God is manifested. It is all of God. It is God's eternal home; it is our eternal home; and in that city Christ is indeed all and in all. This is the goal that is set before us. In order to reach that goal, it is as if we have all been put on a racecourse and that is what you find in chapter 12.

The Obstacle Course

The moment we are saved God puts us on a racecourse, and the end of that course is to win Christ—to know Him and the power of His resurrection, to be conformed to His image, and to obtain into the out-resurrection from among the dead. It is a course that every brother and sister has to begin to run as soon as they are saved. It is not a smooth course; it is a course filled with obstacles. We have overcome all these obstacles in order to arrive at the goal and gain the prize of the calling on high.

Salvation is never cheap. It may be free but it is not cheap. In order to save us God had to sacrifice His only begotten Son. He spared not His own Son in order to save us. Our Lord Jesus gave up His life in order to save us. No one took His life from Him; no one can. He said: "I lay down my life and I take it up." Salvation is very expensive. It is so expensive that you just cannot pay for it, and because it is beyond your payment God has given it to you freely. But it is not cheap.

Dear brothers and sisters, after we have received the Lord Jesus and are put on that racecourse, do we think Christian life is cheap? Not at all! Christian life is very expensive. It is costly because we have to run an obstacle course in order to arrive at the goal. It is not for those who are faint-hearted.

How should we run that race? We have to lay aside every weight. Weight is different from sin. Sin is something that easily entangles us and in Hebrews 12 we are told to cast it aside. You notice "the sin" there is singular number. In other words, there is "the sin" and the sin that easily entangles us in our racing is the sin of unbelief. We have to cast it aside and then lay aside every weight. Weight is not sin, but it is weight, and it will weigh you down so you are not able to run well.

Have you ever seen a runner? When he is going to run, does he put on heavy boots, a fur coat, and all kinds of weight? No, a runner will strip himself of everything that can be stripped in order that he may run. That is what we are all called to do. We are not only to cast away the sin that easily entangles us, but we are to lay aside every weight, anything that will slow us down. It may not be sin, maybe it is the world, but we have to lay it down in order that we may run with endurance. It is an endurance race, not a hundred yard dash. It is not even a cross-country race, but a lifetime race.

We are racing toward the goal, and all the time we are looking away from everything but Jesus, the Author and Finisher of our faith. As we are running and we try to look around, it slows us down. Let our eyes be fixed upon the Lord Jesus. It is a difficult race and only by setting our eyes upon the Lord Jesus, only by thinking about Him, by considering Him, are we able to endure the race. We think of our Lord Jesus—how He ran, how He despised the shame and endured the cross for the joy that was set before Him. We remember how He fought against sin even unto death, shedding His blood. We have not shed our blood yet. Let us take courage and press on.

It is true that the enemy is trying every way to hinder us, to discourage us, to stop us, to turn us aside. It is true that we have to suffer; but thank God, through the things which we suffer, we learn obedience. And all the time we remember that our heavenly Father allows all these hardships and difficulties, and sometimes problems that cannot be explained, to happen in our life-course to child-train us. He wants us to grow up. He wants to have His own character developed in us that we may be partakers of His holiness. Therefore, may we remember these, and lift up the hands that hang down.

PURSUING AFTER CHRIST

"Wherefore lift up the hands that hang down, and the failing knees; and make straight paths for your feet, that that which is lame be not turned aside; but that rather it may be healed. Pursue peace with all, and holiness, without which no one shall see the Lord" (Hebrews 12:12-14). In pressing on toward the goal, the prize of the calling on high, negatively we need to lift up the hands that hang down, strengthen the failing knees, and straighten our paths. Positively, we need to pursue peace with all and holiness. The word *pursue* is very meaningful. You do not pursue without any goal. If there is no goal you are wandering, not pursuing. If you are pursuing, you must pursue after something and we are to pursue. The Christian life is not a life of loafing or wandering; it is not an aimless life. The Christian life is very purposeful. We are pursuing after something. As a matter of fact, we are pursuing after Someone—Christ.

Pursue Peace with All and Holiness

Why are these two things especially mentioned—peace and holiness? Probably it is because as we are running this difficult course we feel it is so hard that we may begin to faint and lose our peace. As we are struggling and striving, as we are trying to press on, sometimes our eyes get off the Lord Jesus and we begin to look at ourselves. We begin to feel how strenuously we are trying. We are trying our best and yet we are getting nowhere. We get frustrated and we begin to lose our peace with

God. We may even begin to murmur against God: "Why is God making it so hard for me?"

Sometimes we look at other people who seem to have a much easier time than we are and because of that we get very jealous. Or in the pursuing we become so ambitious, so competitive that we want to be above everybody, and when we see somebody who has gone ahead of us we become very envious and jealous of them. Or we might run ahead of other people and begin to be very proud of ourselves and look down upon our brothers and sisters who move so slowly. We lose peace with them, and yet the One whom we are pursuing is the Prince of peace. In other words, in this pursuing it is very easy to get lost, but the very purpose of pursuing is to take on the character of the One whom we pursue. What is the sense of achieving if we are not developing His character in us?

Sometimes we see people who are really pursuing and they think they have found the truth or some truth. They begin to be so proud of themselves that they give people the feeling: "We are holier than you are." They begin to look down upon their fellow-citizens, their brothers and sisters. Dear brothers and sisters, is it worth it? They lose the character of the One whom they pursue, and what is it that they get? a little truth, some interpretation? It is nothing! It is the character of Christ that has to be built within us in the pursuing, because He is the One whom we pursue.

We are told to pursue peace and holiness because His very nature is holy. Our Lord is holy. Holy means uncommon. It is different. It is not natural; it is supernatural. It is not you and me; it is HE. It is all of Him. We are pursuing after holiness because without holiness no one can see God. The word "holiness" literally means "holy-making." In other words, we are to be made holy. We are to be made like Him; or to put it another way, we are to be transformed and conformed to His image. We are to let Him be our character; let Him characterize us. This is what holiness really means: "Not I, but Christ."

We are to pursue after that holiness that we may be made partakers of His holiness, that we may yield the fruit of peaceful righteousness.

Isn't that wonderful? Righteousness can be a righteousness that is not peaceful. Sometimes people can be over-righteous and when you are over-righteous it is not peaceful at all, but here it is peaceful righteousness and holiness.

FALLING SHORT OF THE GRACE OF GOD

This is our goal—HIM. Because of this you will find a triple warning immediately following: "Watching lest there be any one who lacks the grace of God" (Hebrews 12:15a). The word *lacks* means "falling short." Watch lest there be anyone who falls short of the grace of God. Isn't it wonderful that we all have the grace of God?

What is the grace of God? The grace of God, on the one hand, is what He has called us to and the grace of God, on the other hand, is what He has supplied us with. His grace calls us into all that He is and then His grace supplies us with all that we need to enter in. You are saved by grace through faith. It is already here and is with every one of us. The grace of God has called us into all that He is for us and the grace of God has supplied us with all the energy, all the strength, all the power that we need to enter into Him. It is all given to us. All we need is: "by grace through faith." In other words, believe...take it...respond to it...receive it.

If you do not respond to grace calling and if you do not receive grace supplying, then you fall short of the grace of God. The grace of God is there, but you are not able to enjoy it. You fall short of it and if you fall short of it there is no excuse. You cannot excuse yourself and say, "It is because I do not know what He has called me to." You cannot say, "It is because I have not found any supply from Him." No, He has already shown you, He has already given to you, but you do not receive it by faith. There will be no excuse.

But thank God, it is just "fall *short* of the grace of God"; it is not "fall *out* of the grace of God." In Galatians 5:4 it is: fall out of the grace of God." That is serious, most serious. To fall short of the grace of God means that you do not arrive at what God has called you to. You become lazy, you are contented with the little that you have, you belittle God, you despise His calling and you do not reach out to rely upon His grace that is sufficient for your every need. If you are doing that you will fall short of the grace of God. Be careful about that.

The Root of Bitterness

"Lest any root of bitterness springing up trouble you, and many be defiled by it (Hebrews 12:15b). It is very strange, but usually those who fall short of the grace of God will find the root of bitterness in them. If you really embrace the grace of God, you will find within you worship and praise. But when you fall short of the grace of God, you begin to blame God as if it is all His fault. The root of bitterness begins to arise within you.

Look at the history of the children of Israel. Because they did not apprehend the grace of God, they turned against God and murmured against Him. Even in Matthew 25, that wicked servant was lazy and wicked. He did not want to work with the talent the master had given to him so he buried it. When he faced the master, he blamed him and said: "You are a hard master." That is the root of bitterness.

But dear brothers and sisters, the problem is that if the root of bitterness arises in your heart, it will not only affect you, but many will be defiled because we are one body. It is a corporate thing. We are running together. It is a team effort, and if any one of us should be bitter soon it will spread to the others. It is just like murmuring. If there is a little murmur somewhere, maybe at an extremity of the camp, it will gradually travel; and because it travels faster than light, it will enter into even the center of the camp until the whole camp begins to cry. Many will be defiled. It is a tremendous privilege to be a member of the body of Christ, but it is a very serious responsibility too. We are responsible not only for ourselves, but we are responsible for our fellow members of the body of Christ. Be careful that we edify people and not offend them.

Losing the Blessing of the Birthright

"Lest there be any fornicator, or profane person, as Esau, who for one meal sold his birthright" (Hebrews 12:16). The word *profane* is the very opposite of holy. Profane simply means "instead of being set apart for God, instead of being sanctified, instead of being uncommon, we become common, we mingle with the world, we love the world, we become one of them." That is profane—like Esau. For the love of one meal, which was not a luxurious dinner but just a snack, a bowl of soup, he sold his birthright. And because he sold his birthright he could not get the blessing connected with it.

Dear brothers and sisters, we have a birthright. Do you know that the church is the assembly of the firstborn whose names are registered in heaven? Because our Lord Jesus is the firstborn, therefore the church is the church of the firstborn. We all have that firstborn right in Christ Jesus. We are all priests and kings. We all have a double portion. That is our birthright. That is the blessing that goes with our birthright, but we may lose the blessing of the birthright if we become profane, if we love the world instead of loving Him—Christ our Lord.

Then we are further encouraged because the writer to the Hebrews tells us we are not coming to Mount Sinai but we have come to Mount Zion.

There is a contrast here between two mountains—Mount Sinai and Mount Zion. It is a contrast between law and grace.

What is Mount Sinai? It is law, and therefore the description of Mount Sinai is that it is a mountain that can be touched. It is physical, but whoever touches it must be stoned to death. It can be touched but if you touch it, it will mean death. It was a terrible sight—all on fire, obscurity, darkness, tempest, trumpet sound, voice of words. When the children of Israel saw this terrible sight when the law was given, they trembled and they begged Moses saying, "Do not let God talk with us lest we die. Let Him talk to you and you tell us." Even Moses said it was so terrible that he was in fear and trembling. This is what law is. Law says, "Thou shall," and "thou shalt not," and can you bear it? Can you hear it without fear and trembling? When you touch the law, you touch death.

But thank God, we do not come to Mount Sinai, we "have come to Mount Zion" and the Mount Zion here is not the Zion in Jerusalem below; it is the Zion in heaven. We are coming to

Mount Zion where God Reigns. We are coming to the city of the Living God, heavenly Jerusalem, where God dwells among His redeemed. We are coming to myriads of angels, the universal gathering. God has myriads of angels ministering to those who are redeemed and praising God, to the assembly of the firstborn who are registered in heaven. That is the church. We are coming to God, Judge of all. We can stand before the Judge of all with holy boldness because of the blood of the Lamb. We are coming to the spirits of just men made perfect. These may be the saints in Old Testament times. They are spirits of just men made perfect. And thank God, we are coming to Jesus, Mediator of a New Covenant. He gave us the New Covenant—our Lord Jesus. And we come to the blood of sprinkling. It is not only the blood poured, but it is the blood sprinkled; it is the blood applied. We are coming to grace.

"Ye have come." We may think the holy city is still in the future, but even though one day the holy city, the New Jerusalem, will descend from above and yet the Bible says, "Ye have come." In spiritual reality, there is no time factor. It is true that one day the holy city will come down from heaven, but spiritually, we have already come. We are already in the holy city. We have already received grace.

Brothers and sisters, do you not know that we are children of grace, not children of law? We are not under law, but we are under grace. Do not think because it is grace and not law, therefore we can be careless. Our human mentality is very strange. If we think we are under law, we know we have to be careful; but, no matter how careful we are we violate the law. However, when we think we are under grace, then we are free to do anything we like because after all, it is grace. Let us not cheat ourselves, because grace is so much greater than law; therefore, our responsibility toward grace is so much greater than to law.

"See that ye refuse not him that speaks. For if those did not escape who had refused him who uttered the oracles on earth, much more we who turn away from him who does so from heaven: whose voice then shook the earth; but now he has promised, saying, Yet once will I shake not only the earth, but also the heaven" (Hebrews 12:25, 26)

We have come to grace, to the grace of God, and the grace of God is none other than Christ. We have come to Christ. Therefore, let us not refuse Him that speaks. God has spoken. He spoke in the past to our fathers through the prophets in bits and pieces, but now He has spoken to us in His own Son. God has spoken. He has spoken to us in His Son. Let us not refuse Him who speaks to us. Let us not excuse ourselves like the children of Israel excused themselves from hearing. Let us not decline from hearing His voice. If people refuse to hear him who speaks the oracle of God on earth, that is Moses, they will die. How much more if we turn away from Him who speaks to us from heaven—Christ. We are warned from turning away from Him. If we turn away from Him, how serious that must be.

A Kingdom that Cannot Be Shaken

"Wherefore let us, receiving a kingdom not to be shaken, have grace, by which let us serve God acceptably with reverence and fear. For also our God is a consuming fire" (Hebrews 12:28, 29).

Here we are being exhorted and encouraged again. Let us not turn away; let us not decline. Let us not refuse to hear Him; but rather let us, receiving a kingdom not to be shaken, have grace. Do you know that it is the good pleasure of our Father to give us the kingdom? The Lord Jesus said in Luke 12: "Fear not little flock (The little flock means the church because the church in comparison with the world is a little flock.) for it is the good pleasure of your Father to give you the kingdom." It is the delight of our heavenly Father to give us the kingdom, and that kingdom is a kingdom that cannot be shaken.

Look at the kingdoms today. All the kingdoms of the world can be shaken. Many have been shaken, many are being shaken, and eventually all will be shaken; but thank God, He has given us a kingdom that cannot be shaken. He has promised us. He has given to us and because He has given to us a kingdom that cannot be shaken, let us have grace.

By Grace Through Faith

"Let us...have grace." What does this mean? If grace has not been given, you cannot have it; but, if grace has already been given, why not have it. In other words, just rise up and take it by faith. Again you find the principle: "by grace through faith." Grace has been given. We have come into Mount Zion; we have come to grace. Let us rise up and take it by faith believing that grace is for us, believing that He has called us to the unshakeable kingdom, and believing that He has sufficient grace to supply us that we may enter into the kingdom abundantly. Believing that, let us take grace by which we can "serve God acceptably with reverence and fear." There is only one way to serve God and that is by His grace. We cannot serve God in ourselves. We cannot serve God by our own cleverness, by our own ingenuity, by our own strength, by our natural life, our natural energy. No. It will be completely rejected by God. The only way we can serve God is by His grace. This is the only service He will accept. It has to be Christ—Christ in you.

"And let us serve with reverence and fear." That is our attitude. We are always afraid lest our own selves, our flesh will intrude, lest we will stretch out the hand of the flesh and be smitten. It is grace from the beginning to the end; it is all of grace. It is grace, grace, amazing grace. Everything is grace, and grace is Christ. He is our goal, He is our supply and He is everything. Because of this, at the very end of this letter to the Hebrews there is a prayer: "But the God of peace, who brought again from among the dead our Lord Jesus, the great shepherd of the sheep, in the power of the blood of the eternal covenant, perfect you in every good work to the doing of his will, doing in you what is pleasing before him through Jesus Christ; to whom be glory for the ages of ages. Amen" (Hebrews 13:20, 21).

God has already demonstrated His grace in Christ Jesus. He has brought again from among the dead our Lord Jesus, the great shepherd of the sheep, in the power of the blood of the eternal covenant. God has demonstrated and expressed His grace in Christ Jesus and in all that Christ has done for us. Now He is going to do all these through Christ Jesus by the Holy Spirit in each one of us that He may perfect us in every good work in the doing of His will, doing in you what is pleasing before Him through Jesus Christ. It is not only what Christ has done on Calvary's cross, but it is "Christ in you, the hope of glory," and again it is all His doing.

In the book of Hebrews we have all these wonderful things before us—SO GREAT SALVATION, HEAVENLY CALLING, PERFECTION, LIFE IN THE HOLIEST, GOAL AND THE PRIZE OF THE HIGH CALLING. All this is what grace is calling us to, but at the same time this very same grace is in each one of us to supply us with everything that is needed for us to arrive at the goal. It is He who does it, not you. All that you need to do is believe and cooperate. May the Lord help us. To Him be the glory from the ages to the ages. Amen.

Shall we pray:

Dear heavenly Father, how we do praise and thank Thee that what Thou hast done in Christ

Jesus and called us into is not a small thing, but it is so tremendous that it is really beyond our understanding. But we praise and thank Thee that by Thy Holy Spirit it is revealed to us and continually revealed to us. And Father, we pray that we may not be those who are of faint heart but those who will rise up by Thy grace and apprehend Thy grace by faith that we may find that Thy grace which calls us is the grace that keeps us. And Father we do pray that truly it may be all unto the praise of Thy glory. In the name of our Lord Jesus. Amen.

Other Books Printed By Christian Testimony Ministry

Speaker	Title
Dana Congdon	Marriage, Singleness, and the Will of God
	Recovery & Restoration
	The Holy Spirit
	Hebrews
A.J. Flack	Tent of His Splendour
Stephen Kaung	Acts
	Be Ye Therefore Perfect
	Called Out Unto Christ
	Called to the Fellowship of God's Son
	Divine Life and Order
	For Me to Live is Christ
	Glorious Liberty of the Children of God
	God's Purpose for the Family
	I Will Build My Church
	Meditations on the Kingdom
	Recovery
	Spiritual Exercise
	Spiritual Life (II Corinthians Series)
	Teach Us to Pray
	The Cross
	The Fulness of Christ—In the Book of Revelation
	The Headship of Christ
	The Kingdom and the Church
	The Kingdom of God
	The Last Call to the Churches, the Call to Overcome
	The Life of Our Lord Jesus
	The Life of the Church, the Body of Christ
	The Lord's Table
	Two Guideposts for Inheriting the Kingdom
	Vision of Christ (Revelation)
	Who Are We?

	Why Do We So Gather?
	Worship
Lance Lambert	Called Unto His Eternal Glory
	God's Eternal Purpose
	In the Day of Thy Power
	Jacob I Have Loved
	Living Faith
	Lessons from the Life of Moses
	Love Divine
	My House Shall be a House of Prayer
	Preparation for the Coming of the Lord
	Reigning with Christ
	Spiritual Character
	The Gospel of the Kingdom
	The Importance of Covering
	The Last Days and God's Priorities
	The Prize
	The Supremacy of Jesus Christ
	Thine is the Power!
	Thou Art Mine
T. Austin-Sparks	The Lord's Testimony and the World Need

Harvey Cedars Conference

Stephen Kaung	Heavenly Vision
	Spiritual Responsibility
Congdon, Hile, Kaung	Spiritual Ministry
	Spiritual Authority
	Spiritual House
	Spiritual Submission
Stephen Kaung	Spiritual Knowledge
	Spiritual Power
	Spiritual Reality
	Spiritual Value
	Spiritual Blessing
	Spiritual Discernment

Spiritual Warfare
Spiritual Ascendancy
Spiritual Mindedness
Spiritual Perfection
Spiritual Fulness
Spiritual Sonship
Spiritual Stewardship
Spiritual Travail
Spiritual Inheritance
Harvey Cedars Conference:
Hile, Kaung, Lambert
The King is Coming

www.ingramcontent.com/pod-product-compliance
Lightning Source LLC
Chambersburg PA
CBHW051042030426
42339CB00006B/150
* 9 7 8 1 9 4 2 5 2 1 0 2 0 *